55 Egyptian Recipes for Home

By: Kelly Johnson

Table of Contents

Appetizers:

- Hummus with Tahini
- Baba Ganoush
- Koshari Bites (Mini Koshari)
- Foul Medames (Fava Bean Dip)
- Warak Enab (Stuffed Grape Leaves)
- Taameya (Egyptian Falafel)
- Eggah (Egyptian Omelette)
- Herring Salad (Salatit Sill)
- Roz Bel Laban (Rice Pudding with Milk)

Main Courses:

- Koshari (Lentils, Rice, and Pasta Dish)
- Molokhia (Jute Leaf Stew)
- Mahshi (Stuffed Vegetables)
- Fattah (Layered Bread Dish)
- Hawawshi (Meat-Stuffed Pita)
- Samak Meshwi (Grilled Fish)
- Bamia (Okra Stew)
- Macarona Bechamel (Egyptian Baked Pasta)
- Kushari Lasagna

Street Food:

- Shawarma
- Hawawshi (Meat Pie)
- Tameya Sandwich (Falafel Sandwich)
- Baladi Bread with Cheese and Herbs

Side Dishes:

- Egyptian Pickles
- Torshi (Pickled Vegetables)

- Egyptian Lentil Soup
- Dukkah (Nut and Spice Blend)

Desserts:

- Basbousa (Semolina Cake)
- Umm Ali (Bread Pudding)
- Roz Bel Laban w Nataf (Rice Pudding with Coconut)
- Qatayef (Stuffed Pancakes)
- Kunafa (Middle Eastern Pastry)
- Aish El Saraya (Bread Pudding with Custard)
- Ghorayeba (Butter Cookies)

Beverages:

- Hibiscus Tea (Karkadeh)
- Sahlab (Warm Milk Pudding)
- Sobia (Coconut Drink)
- Tamarind Juice (Tamr Hindi)
- Qamar al-Din (Apricot Juice)
- Mint Lemonade (Limonana)

Grilled Dishes:

- Shish Kebab
- Kofta (Minced Meat Skewers)

Vegetarian Delights:

- Koshari (Vegetarian Version)
- Lentil Kebabs (Kebdet Adas)

Traditional Sweets:

- Roz Bel Laban (Rice Pudding)
- Basbousa with Pistachios
- Atayef (Stuffed Pancakes)
- Kunafa with Nuts

Seafood Specialities:

- Sayadiya (Fish and Rice Dish)
- Fried Fish with Tarator Sauce

Special Occasion Dishes:

- Mulukhiyah with Rabbit
- Fattah with Lamb

Spicy Delicacies:

- Hawawshi (Spicy Meat Pie)
- Kebsa (Spicy Rice with Meat)
- Shatta (Hot Pepper Sauce)

Miscellaneous:

- Aish Merahrah (Red Lentil Bread)

Appetizers:

Hummus with Tahini

Ingredients:

- 1 can (15 oz) chickpeas, drained and rinsed (or 1 1/2 cups cooked chickpeas)
- 1/3 cup tahini
- 1/4 cup extra virgin olive oil, plus extra for drizzling
- 1 clove garlic, minced
- 1 teaspoon ground cumin
- 1/2 teaspoon salt, or to taste
- Juice of 1 lemon
- 2 to 3 tablespoons water (to achieve desired consistency)
- Optional garnishes: paprika, chopped fresh parsley

Instructions:

Prepare Chickpeas:
- If using canned chickpeas, drain and rinse them thoroughly. If using dried chickpeas, cook and cool them according to package instructions.

Combine Ingredients:
- In a food processor, combine the chickpeas, tahini, olive oil, minced garlic, ground cumin, salt, and lemon juice.

Blend Until Smooth:
- Process the ingredients until smooth. Stop and scrape down the sides of the bowl as needed to ensure an even consistency.

Adjust Consistency:
- While the food processor is running, add water one tablespoon at a time until the hummus reaches your desired creamy consistency.

Taste and Adjust Seasoning:
- Taste the hummus and adjust the salt and lemon juice according to your preference. Blend again to incorporate any adjustments.

Serve:
- Transfer the hummus to a serving bowl. Create a shallow well in the center with the back of a spoon and drizzle with extra virgin olive oil. Optionally, sprinkle with paprika and chopped fresh parsley for garnish.

Enjoy:

- Serve the classic hummus with tahini with pita bread, vegetable sticks, or your favorite crackers. It also makes a delicious spread for sandwiches or wraps.

Storage:
- Store any leftovers in an airtight container in the refrigerator. Hummus can be refrigerated for up to a week.

This classic hummus recipe with tahini provides a versatile base that you can customize with additional ingredients or toppings according to your taste preferences.

Baba Ganoush

Ingredients:

- 2 large eggplants
- 1/4 cup tahini
- 2 cloves garlic, minced
- 2 tablespoons extra virgin olive oil, plus extra for drizzling
- Juice of 1 lemon
- 1/2 teaspoon ground cumin
- 1/2 teaspoon smoked paprika
- Salt and pepper, to taste
- 2 tablespoons fresh parsley, chopped (for garnish)
- Optional: Pomegranate seeds for garnish

Instructions:

Roast the Eggplants:
- Preheat the oven to 400°F (200°C). Pierce the eggplants with a fork in a few places. Place them on a baking sheet and roast in the oven for about 45-50 minutes or until the skin is charred, and the flesh is soft.

Cool and Peel:
- Allow the roasted eggplants to cool. Once cooled, peel off the charred skin, leaving only the soft flesh. Discard the skin.

Drain Excess Moisture:
- Place the peeled eggplant in a colander to drain excess moisture for about 10-15 minutes.

Blend Ingredients:
- In a food processor, combine the drained eggplant, tahini, minced garlic, olive oil, lemon juice, ground cumin, smoked paprika, salt, and pepper.

Blend Until Smooth:
- Process the ingredients until smooth. Stop and scrape down the sides of the bowl as needed to ensure an even consistency.

Adjust Seasoning:
- Taste the baba ganoush and adjust the seasoning, adding more salt, pepper, or lemon juice if necessary. Blend again to incorporate any adjustments.

Chill:

- Transfer the baba ganoush to a serving bowl. Cover and refrigerate for at least 1-2 hours to allow the flavors to meld.

Serve:
- Before serving, drizzle with extra virgin olive oil and garnish with chopped fresh parsley. Optionally, add a sprinkle of pomegranate seeds for a burst of color and flavor.

Enjoy:
- Serve the baba ganoush with pita bread, vegetable sticks, or as a side dish. It can also be a delightful spread for sandwiches or wraps.

Storage:
- Store any leftover baba ganoush in an airtight container in the refrigerator. It can be refrigerated for up to a week.

This baba ganoush recipe provides a silky and smoky eggplant dip, perfect for sharing as an appetizer or enjoying as a flavorful accompaniment to your meals.

Koshari Bites (Mini Koshari)

Ingredients:

For the Lentils:

- 1/2 cup brown lentils, rinsed
- 2 cups water
- Salt to taste

For the Rice:

- 1 cup basmati rice
- 2 cups water
- Salt to taste

For the Pasta:

- 1/2 cup short pasta (e.g., elbow macaroni)
- Water for boiling
- Salt to taste

For the Tomato Sauce:

- 1 can (14 oz) crushed tomatoes
- 2 cloves garlic, minced
- 1 teaspoon ground cumin
- 1 teaspoon ground coriander
- 1/2 teaspoon cayenne pepper (adjust to taste)
- Salt and pepper to taste
- 2 tablespoons olive oil

For the Fried Onions:

- 1 large onion, thinly sliced
- Vegetable oil for frying

For Assembly:

- Cooked chickpeas (canned or cooked from dry)

- Cooked green or brown lentils (optional)
- Chopped fresh parsley for garnish
- White vinegar (optional, for serving)

Instructions:

Prepare Lentils:
- In a saucepan, combine the rinsed brown lentils, water, and salt. Bring to a boil, then reduce heat and simmer until lentils are tender but not mushy. Drain any excess water.

Cook Rice:
- Rinse basmati rice under cold water until the water runs clear. In a separate pot, bring water to a boil, add salt and rice. Cook until the rice is fluffy. Set aside.

Boil Pasta:
- Cook the short pasta in boiling salted water until al dente. Drain and set aside.

Prepare Tomato Sauce:
- In a saucepan, heat olive oil. Add minced garlic and sauté until fragrant. Add crushed tomatoes, cumin, coriander, cayenne pepper, salt, and pepper. Simmer for 15-20 minutes until the sauce thickens. Adjust seasoning if needed.

Fry Onions:
- In a frying pan, heat vegetable oil over medium-high heat. Fry thinly sliced onions until golden and crispy. Remove from oil and place on a paper towel to drain excess oil.

Assemble Koshari Bites:
- In a serving platter or individual appetizer plates, layer the mini koshari bites. Start with a base of cooked lentils, followed by rice, then pasta. Spoon tomato sauce over the layers.

Top with Chickpeas and Lentils:
- Add cooked chickpeas and, if desired, some cooked green or brown lentils on top of the tomato sauce layer.

Garnish:
- Sprinkle fried onions generously over the koshari bites. Garnish with chopped fresh parsley.

Serve:
- Optionally, serve with a side of white vinegar for drizzling.

Enjoy:

- Serve these mini koshari bites as a delightful appetizer, or make a full meal by pairing them with a side salad. Enjoy the flavors of this Egyptian street food classic in bite-sized form!

These mini koshari bites capture the essence of the traditional dish in a convenient and appetizing form, perfect for entertaining or as a unique addition to your appetizer menu.

Foul Medames (Fava Bean Dip)

Ingredients:

For the Fava Beans:

- 2 cups dried fava beans
- Water for soaking
- Water for cooking
- Salt to taste

For the Fava Bean Dip:

- 1/4 cup olive oil
- 1 onion, finely chopped
- 3 cloves garlic, minced
- 1 teaspoon ground cumin
- 1 teaspoon ground coriander
- 1/2 teaspoon ground paprika
- Salt and pepper to taste
- Juice of 1 lemon
- Fresh parsley, chopped, for garnish
- Optional toppings: diced tomatoes, radishes, cucumbers, and hard-boiled eggs

Instructions:

Soak and Cook Fava Beans:
- Rinse the dried fava beans thoroughly and soak them in water overnight. Drain and rinse again. In a large pot, cover the soaked fava beans with water and bring to a boil. Reduce the heat and simmer until the beans are tender, adding more water if necessary. Add salt towards the end of the cooking time. The beans should be soft but not mushy. Drain any excess water.

Prepare Fava Bean Dip:
- In a large skillet, heat olive oil over medium heat. Add finely chopped onions and sauté until translucent.

Add Aromatics:

- Stir in minced garlic and sauté until fragrant. Add ground cumin, ground coriander, and ground paprika. Mix well and cook for an additional 1-2 minutes.

Mash Fava Beans:
- Add the cooked fava beans to the skillet. Using a potato masher or the back of a spoon, mash the beans to your desired consistency. Some prefer a smoother texture, while others enjoy a chunkier dip.

Season and Finish:
- Season the mixture with salt and pepper. Squeeze the juice of one lemon into the mix and stir well. Cook for an additional 5-7 minutes, allowing the flavors to meld.

Garnish and Serve:
- Transfer the Foul Medames to a serving bowl. Garnish with chopped fresh parsley and any optional toppings you desire, such as diced tomatoes, radishes, cucumbers, or hard-boiled eggs.

Drizzle with Olive Oil:
- Before serving, drizzle a bit of extra virgin olive oil over the top for added richness and flavor.

Serve Warm:
- Foul Medames is traditionally served warm. Enjoy it as a dip with pita bread or crusty bread, or as a side dish with additional toppings.

Optional Variation - Foul Medames Salad:
- For a refreshing twist, let the Foul Medames cool, and toss it with chopped tomatoes, cucumbers, onions, and fresh herbs to create a flavorful salad.

Enjoy:
- Whether served as a dip or salad, Foul Medames makes for a satisfying and nutritious dish, showcasing the rich flavors of fava beans and aromatic spices.

Warak Enab (Stuffed Grape Leaves)

Ingredients:

For the Grape Leaves:

- 1 jar of grape leaves in brine, rinsed and drained
- Water for soaking

For the Rice Filling:

- 1 cup short-grain rice
- 1 medium-sized onion, finely chopped
- 2 tablespoons olive oil
- 1/4 cup pine nuts (optional)
- 1/2 teaspoon ground cinnamon
- 1/2 teaspoon ground allspice
- Salt and pepper to taste

For the Stuffing Mixture:

- Juice of 2 lemons
- 2 tablespoons olive oil
- 1 cup hot water
- 1 teaspoon sugar

For Cooking:

- Water or vegetable broth for boiling
- Extra virgin olive oil for drizzling

Instructions:

> Prepare Grape Leaves:
> - If using grape leaves preserved in brine, rinse them thoroughly in cold water to remove excess salt. Soak the leaves in warm water for about 10-15 minutes to soften.
>
> Prepare Rice Filling:

- In a skillet, heat olive oil over medium heat. Sauté finely chopped onions until translucent. Add pine nuts (if using) and continue to sauté until they are lightly toasted.

Add Rice and Spices:
- Stir in the short-grain rice and cook for an additional 2-3 minutes until the rice is lightly toasted. Add ground cinnamon, ground allspice, salt, and pepper. Mix well.

Cook Rice:
- Pour in enough water to cover the rice by about an inch. Bring to a boil, then reduce heat to low, cover, and simmer until the rice is cooked and has absorbed the water. Remove from heat and let it cool.

Prepare Stuffing Mixture:
- In a separate bowl, combine the lemon juice, olive oil, hot water, and sugar. Mix well to create the stuffing mixture.

Assemble Stuffed Grape Leaves:
- Lay a grape leaf flat on a clean surface, vein side up. Trim or remove the stem if necessary. Place a small spoonful of the rice filling in the center of the leaf.

Rolling Technique:
- Fold the sides of the grape leaf over the filling and then roll it tightly from the bottom to the top, creating a compact cylinder.

Repeat:
- Repeat the process with the remaining grape leaves and rice filling.

Layer in Cooking Pot:
- In a wide pot, arrange the stuffed grape leaves snugly, seam side down, in layers. Place a few grape leaves on the bottom of the pot to prevent sticking.

Add Stuffing Mixture:
- Pour the stuffing mixture over the stuffed grape leaves. Place a heavy plate or an inverted heat-resistant dish on top to keep the grape leaves from unraveling during cooking.

Cooking:
- Add water or vegetable broth to the pot until it covers the stuffed grape leaves. Bring to a gentle boil, then reduce heat to low, cover, and simmer for about 45-60 minutes or until the grape leaves are tender and the rice is fully cooked.

Serve:

- Once cooked, let the stuffed grape leaves cool slightly. Arrange them on a serving platter, drizzle with extra virgin olive oil, and serve at room temperature or slightly warm.

Enjoy:

- Warak Enab makes for a delicious appetizer or part of a mezze spread. Serve with a side of yogurt or tahini sauce for a delightful Middle Eastern dish.

Taameya (Egyptian Falafel)

Ingredients:

For the Falafel:

- 1 cup dried fava beans, soaked overnight
- 1/2 cup dried chickpeas, soaked overnight
- 1 small onion, roughly chopped
- 3 cloves garlic
- 1 cup fresh parsley, chopped
- 1 cup fresh cilantro, chopped
- 1 teaspoon ground cumin
- 1 teaspoon ground coriander
- 1 teaspoon baking soda
- Salt and pepper to taste

For Frying:

- Vegetable oil for frying

Instructions:

Soak Beans:
- Rinse and soak the dried fava beans and chickpeas in separate bowls overnight. Make sure they are fully covered with water.

Drain and Rinse:
- Drain and rinse the soaked fava beans and chickpeas thoroughly.

Prepare the Falafel Mix:
- In a food processor, combine the soaked and drained fava beans, chickpeas, chopped onion, garlic, parsley, cilantro, ground cumin, ground coriander, baking soda, salt, and pepper.

Blend Until Smooth:
- Process the mixture until you get a coarse paste. You may need to stop and scrape down the sides of the food processor to ensure even blending. The texture should be a coarse mixture rather than a completely smooth puree.

Chill the Mixture:

- Transfer the falafel mixture to a bowl, cover, and refrigerate for at least 1-2 hours. Chilling helps the mixture firm up and makes it easier to shape into balls.

Shape Falafel:
- After chilling, wet your hands and shape the falafel mixture into small balls or patties. You can make them about 1 to 1.5 inches in diameter.

Fry the Falafel:
- In a deep skillet or fryer, heat vegetable oil to 350°F (180°C). Carefully drop the falafel balls into the hot oil, frying until they are golden brown and crispy. Fry in batches to avoid overcrowding the pan.

Drain Excess Oil:
- Use a slotted spoon to remove the fried falafel from the oil, allowing excess oil to drain. Place them on a plate lined with paper towels.

Serve:
- Serve the taameya (Egyptian falafel) hot, either in pita bread with tahini sauce, or as part of a mezze spread with salads and dips.

Optional:
- You can also serve falafel with pickles, fresh tomatoes, cucumbers, and drizzle additional tahini sauce or hot sauce on top for extra flavor.

Enjoy:
- Enjoy these delicious and authentic Egyptian falafel, filled with the flavors of fresh herbs and spices. They make for a fantastic snack or a satisfying addition to a meal.

Eggah (Egyptian Omelette)

Ingredients:

- 6 large eggs
- 1 small onion, finely chopped
- 1 small bell pepper, finely chopped
- 2 tomatoes, diced
- 1/4 cup fresh parsley, chopped
- 1/4 cup fresh cilantro, chopped
- 1/2 teaspoon ground cumin
- Salt and pepper to taste
- 2 tablespoons olive oil

Optional Additions:

- Feta cheese, crumbled
- Olives, sliced
- Sausages or pastrami, diced

Instructions:

Preheat Oven:
- Preheat your oven's broiler.

Prepare Vegetables:
- Finely chop the onion, bell pepper, tomatoes, parsley, and cilantro.

Sauté Vegetables:
- In an oven-safe skillet, heat olive oil over medium heat. Add the chopped onion and bell pepper, sautéing until they are softened.

Add Tomatoes and Herbs:
- Add the diced tomatoes to the skillet, stirring occasionally until they release their juices. Mix in the fresh parsley and cilantro.

Season with Spices:
- Sprinkle ground cumin, salt, and pepper over the vegetables. Adjust the seasoning according to your taste.

Optional Additions:
- If you're adding optional ingredients like feta cheese, olives, or diced sausages, mix them into the vegetable mixture.

Beat Eggs:
- In a separate bowl, beat the eggs until well combined.

Combine Eggs and Vegetables:
- Pour the beaten eggs over the sautéed vegetables in the skillet. Ensure the eggs evenly cover the vegetables.

Cook on Stovetop:
- Cook the mixture on the stovetop over medium heat, allowing the edges to set. Lift the edges gently with a spatula to let the uncooked egg flow underneath.

Finish Under the Broiler:
- Transfer the skillet to the preheated oven's broiler. Allow the top of the eggah to cook and lightly brown under the broiler. Keep a close eye to prevent burning, as this process is quick.

Serve Warm:
- Once the top is set and slightly browned, remove the skillet from the oven. Let it cool for a moment, then slice the eggah into wedges.

Optional Garnish:
- Garnish with additional fresh herbs or a sprinkle of crumbled feta if desired.

Serve:
- Serve the eggah warm as a hearty breakfast, brunch, or a satisfying main course. It pairs well with fresh bread, a side salad, or pickles.

Enjoy:
- Enjoy the delicious flavors of this Egyptian omelette, packed with the goodness of fresh vegetables and herbs.

Herring Salad (Salatit Sill)

Ingredients:

For the Salad:

- 2 cups pickled herring fillets, diced
- 2 large potatoes, boiled and diced
- 2 medium-sized apples, cored and diced
- 1 small red onion, finely chopped
- 1 cup dill pickles, diced
- 1/2 cup cooked beets, diced (optional, for color)
- 1/4 cup capers, drained
- Fresh dill, chopped, for garnish

For the Dressing:

- 1/2 cup sour cream
- 1/4 cup mayonnaise
- 1 tablespoon Dijon mustard
- 1 tablespoon white wine vinegar
- Salt and pepper to taste

Instructions:

Prepare Ingredients:
- Dice the pickled herring, boiled potatoes, apples, red onion, dill pickles, and cooked beets (if using). Set aside.

Make the Dressing:
- In a bowl, whisk together sour cream, mayonnaise, Dijon mustard, white wine vinegar, salt, and pepper. Adjust the seasoning to your taste.

Combine Salad Ingredients:
- In a large mixing bowl, combine the diced herring, potatoes, apples, red onion, pickles, and capers. If using beets, add them as well.

Add Dressing:
- Pour the prepared dressing over the salad ingredients. Gently toss the salad to coat all the ingredients evenly with the dressing.

Chill:
- Cover the bowl and refrigerate the herring salad for at least 1-2 hours to allow the flavors to meld and the salad to chill.

Garnish:
- Before serving, garnish the herring salad with chopped fresh dill.

Serve:
- Serve the Salatit Sill as a refreshing appetizer, side dish, or part of a festive spread. It goes well with crusty bread or crackers.

Enjoy:
- Enjoy the delightful combination of flavors and textures in this herring salad, featuring the briny richness of herring, the creaminess of potatoes, and the sweetness of apples, all brought together with a tangy dressing.

Roz Bel Laban (Rice Pudding with Milk)

Ingredients:

- 1 cup medium-grain rice
- 4 cups whole milk
- 1 cup sugar (adjust to taste)
- 1 teaspoon vanilla extract
- 1/2 cup heavy cream (optional, for added richness)
- Ground cinnamon or nutmeg for garnish
- Chopped nuts (such as pistachios or almonds) for garnish

Instructions:

Rinse and Soak Rice:
- Rinse the rice under cold water until the water runs clear. Soak the rice in water for about 30 minutes to 1 hour.

Cook Rice:
- In a heavy-bottomed saucepan, combine the soaked rice and 2 cups of milk. Bring to a simmer over medium heat, then reduce the heat to low. Cook the rice, stirring occasionally, until it absorbs most of the milk and becomes soft and creamy.

Add Sugar and Vanilla:
- Add the sugar and vanilla extract to the rice, stirring well to combine. Continue to cook on low heat, allowing the sugar to dissolve and the rice to absorb more liquid.

Incorporate Remaining Milk:
- Gradually add the remaining 2 cups of milk, stirring continuously to prevent the rice from sticking to the bottom of the pan. Allow the mixture to simmer on low heat until the rice is fully cooked and the pudding thickens to your desired consistency.

Optional Heavy Cream:
- If using heavy cream, stir it into the rice pudding for added richness. Cook for an additional 5-10 minutes.

Check Sweetness:
- Taste the rice pudding and adjust the sweetness according to your preference by adding more sugar if needed. Keep in mind that the pudding will sweeten a bit as it cools.

Cool and Chill:

- Remove the rice pudding from heat and let it cool for a bit. Then, transfer it to serving bowls or a large dish. Cover with plastic wrap directly touching the surface of the pudding to prevent a skin from forming. Chill in the refrigerator for at least 2-3 hours or overnight.

Garnish and Serve:
- Before serving, sprinkle ground cinnamon or nutmeg on top of the chilled rice pudding. Garnish with chopped nuts, such as pistachios or almonds.

Enjoy:
- Serve Roz Bel Laban cold as a delightful dessert. It's a comforting and creamy rice pudding that is perfect for any occasion.

Main Courses:

Koshari (Lentils, Rice, and Pasta Dish)

Ingredients:

For the Lentils:

- 1 cup brown or green lentils, rinsed
- 4 cups water
- Salt to taste

For the Rice:

- 1 cup basmati rice
- 2 cups water
- Salt to taste

For the Pasta:

- 1 cup small pasta (e.g., elbow macaroni or ditalini)
- Water for boiling
- Salt to taste

For the Tomato Sauce:

- 1 can (14 oz) crushed tomatoes
- 2 cloves garlic, minced
- 1 teaspoon ground cumin
- 1 teaspoon ground coriander
- 1/2 teaspoon cayenne pepper (adjust to taste)
- Salt and pepper to taste
- 2 tablespoons olive oil

For the Fried Onions:

- 1 large onion, thinly sliced
- Vegetable oil for frying

For Assembly:

- Cooked lentils
- Cooked rice
- Cooked pasta
- Tomato sauce
- Fried onions
- Chickpeas (canned or cooked from dry), optional
- Vinegar (white or apple cider), optional
- Hot sauce, optional

Instructions:

Prepare Lentils:
- In a saucepan, combine the rinsed lentils, water, and salt. Bring to a boil, then reduce heat and simmer until lentils are tender but not mushy. Drain any excess water.

Cook Rice:
- Rinse basmati rice under cold water until the water runs clear. In a separate pot, bring water to a boil, add salt and rice. Cook until the rice is fluffy. Set aside.

Boil Pasta:
- Cook the small pasta in boiling salted water until al dente. Drain and set aside.

Prepare Tomato Sauce:
- In a saucepan, heat olive oil. Add minced garlic and sauté until fragrant. Add crushed tomatoes, cumin, coriander, cayenne pepper, salt, and pepper. Simmer for 15-20 minutes until the sauce thickens. Adjust seasoning if needed.

Fry Onions:
- In a frying pan, heat vegetable oil over medium-high heat. Fry thinly sliced onions until golden and crispy. Remove from oil and place on a paper towel to drain excess oil.

Assemble Koshari:
- In a serving dish or individual plates, layer the cooked lentils, rice, and pasta. Spoon tomato sauce over the layers. Top with fried onions.

Optional Chickpeas:
- If using chickpeas, add them on top of the layers.

Optional Vinegar:
- Optionally, serve with a side of vinegar (white or apple cider) for drizzling. Some also like to add a splash of hot sauce for extra heat.

Mix and Enjoy:
- Before eating, mix all the layers together. The combination of flavors and textures is key to the deliciousness of Koshari.

Serve:
- Serve Koshari as a satisfying and hearty meal. It's a popular Egyptian street food dish that brings together a variety of ingredients in a flavorful and comforting way.

Molokhia (Jute Leaf Stew)

Ingredients:

For the Molokhia Base:

- 2 cups dried molokhia leaves (jute leaves)
- 4 cups chicken or vegetable broth
- 4 cloves garlic, minced
- 2 tablespoons olive oil
- Salt and pepper to taste

For the Meat (Optional):

- 1 lb chicken, beef, or rabbit (cut into pieces)
- 1 onion, finely chopped
- 2 cloves garlic, minced
- 1 tablespoon vegetable oil
- Salt and pepper to taste

For Serving:

- Cooked rice or bread

For Garnish (Optional):

- Lemon wedges
- Chopped fresh cilantro or parsley

Instructions:

Prepare Molokhia Base:
- Rinse the dried molokhia leaves under cold water. In a pot, sauté minced garlic in olive oil until fragrant. Add the molokhia leaves and stir.

Add Broth:
- Pour in the chicken or vegetable broth. Bring the mixture to a boil, then reduce heat and let it simmer. Season with salt and pepper. Allow the molokhia to simmer until it thickens, stirring occasionally.

Prepare Meat (Optional):

- In a separate pan, sauté chopped onions and minced garlic in vegetable oil until translucent. Add the meat pieces and cook until browned. Season with salt and pepper.

Combine Meat with Molokhia:
- If you're using meat, combine it with the molokhia base. Allow the meat and molokhia to simmer together for additional flavor.

Adjust Seasoning:
- Taste the molokhia and adjust the seasoning if needed. Some prefer to add a bit of lemon juice for extra tanginess.

Serve:
- Serve molokhia over cooked rice or accompanied by bread.

Garnish (Optional):
- Garnish with lemon wedges and chopped fresh cilantro or parsley if desired.

Enjoy:
- Molokhia is typically enjoyed as a warm stew over rice or bread. The dish is rich and comforting, with the distinctive flavor of molokhia leaves. Adjust the consistency to your liking by adding more or less broth.

Mahshi (Stuffed Vegetables)

Ingredients:

For the Filling:

- 1 cup rice, rinsed
- 1/2 lb ground meat (beef or lamb), optional
- 1 onion, finely chopped
- 2 tomatoes, diced
- 1/4 cup tomato paste
- 1/4 cup fresh parsley, chopped
- 1/4 cup fresh dill, chopped
- Salt and pepper to taste
- 1 teaspoon ground allspice
- 1 teaspoon ground cumin

For the Vegetables:

- 8-10 medium-sized vegetables for stuffing (zucchini, eggplants, bell peppers, tomatoes, or grape leaves)
- Lemon juice for drizzling

For Cooking:

- 2 cups vegetable or chicken broth
- Olive oil for drizzling

Instructions:

Prepare the Vegetables:
- For zucchini and eggplants, cut them in half lengthwise and scoop out the centers, leaving a shell. For bell peppers, cut off the tops and remove seeds. For tomatoes, cut a small lid from the top and scoop out the pulp. For grape leaves, carefully remove the stems.

Prepare the Filling:
- In a bowl, combine the rinsed rice, ground meat (if using), chopped onion, diced tomatoes, tomato paste, fresh parsley, fresh dill, salt, pepper, ground allspice, and ground cumin. Mix well.

Stuff the Vegetables:

- Fill each vegetable with the rice and meat mixture. Do not overstuff, as rice will expand during cooking. For grape leaves, place about one tablespoon of the mixture in the center and fold the sides over.

Arrange in a Pot:
- Place the stuffed vegetables in a large pot, arranging them snugly. If there are any empty spaces, you can place grape leaves or small tomato slices to fill the gaps.

Drizzle with Olive Oil:
- Drizzle olive oil over the stuffed vegetables. This adds flavor and helps prevent sticking.

Add Broth:
- Pour vegetable or chicken broth into the pot until it reaches about halfway up the stuffed vegetables.

Cook:
- Cover the pot and bring it to a boil. Reduce heat and let it simmer gently for about 40-50 minutes, or until the rice is fully cooked and the vegetables are tender.

Check Doneness:
- To check if they are done, pierce the vegetables with a fork. If the fork goes through easily, they are ready.

Serve:
- Transfer the stuffed vegetables to a serving platter. Drizzle with lemon juice and olive oil.

Enjoy:
- Mahshi is traditionally served warm or at room temperature. It can be enjoyed as a main dish or part of a mezze spread. Serve with a side of yogurt or tahini sauce if desired.

Fattah (Layered Bread Dish)

Ingredients:

For the Rice:

- 2 cups basmati rice
- 4 cups water
- Salt to taste

For the Bread:

- 4 pieces of flatbread or pita bread, toasted or fried until crispy

For the Meat:

- 1 lb lamb or beef, diced
- 1 onion, finely chopped
- 2 cloves garlic, minced
- 1 teaspoon ground cumin
- 1 teaspoon ground coriander
- Salt and pepper to taste
- 2 tablespoons vegetable oil

For the Tomato Sauce:

- 1 can (14 oz) crushed tomatoes
- 2 cloves garlic, minced
- 1 teaspoon ground cumin
- 1 teaspoon ground coriander
- Salt and pepper to taste
- 2 tablespoons olive oil

For the Yogurt Sauce:

- 2 cups plain yogurt
- 2 cloves garlic, minced
- Salt to taste

For Garnish:

- Chopped fresh parsley or cilantro
- Pine nuts, toasted
- Butter, melted

Instructions:

Prepare the Rice:
- Rinse the basmati rice under cold water until the water runs clear. In a pot, bring water to a boil, add salt and rice. Cook until the rice is fluffy. Set aside.

Prepare the Bread:
- Toast or fry the flatbread or pita until it becomes crispy. Break it into bite-sized pieces.

Cook the Meat:
- In a pan, heat vegetable oil over medium heat. Sauté chopped onions until translucent. Add minced garlic and cook until fragrant. Add diced lamb or beef, ground cumin, ground coriander, salt, and pepper. Cook until the meat is browned.

Make the Tomato Sauce:
- In a separate saucepan, heat olive oil. Add minced garlic and sauté until fragrant. Add crushed tomatoes, ground cumin, ground coriander, salt, and pepper. Simmer for 15-20 minutes until the sauce thickens.

Prepare the Yogurt Sauce:
- Mix plain yogurt with minced garlic and salt. Adjust the seasoning to taste.

Assemble the Fattah:
- In a serving dish, start by layering the crispy bread at the bottom. Pour a portion of the tomato sauce over the bread. Add a layer of cooked rice, followed by the spiced meat.

Repeat Layers:
- Repeat the layering process until you run out of ingredients, finishing with a layer of crispy bread on top.

Top with Yogurt Sauce:
- Pour the yogurt sauce over the top layer of bread.

Garnish:
- Garnish the fattah with chopped fresh parsley or cilantro, toasted pine nuts, and a drizzle of melted butter.

Serve:
- Fattah is traditionally served warm. Allow the flavors to meld before serving.

Enjoy:
- Enjoy this layered bread dish with a delicious combination of flavors and textures. Fattah is often served during special occasions and celebrations.

Hawawshi (Meat-Stuffed Pita)

Ingredients:

For the Meat Filling:

- 1 lb ground beef or lamb
- 1 large onion, finely chopped
- 2 cloves garlic, minced
- 1 medium-sized tomato, finely chopped
- 1/4 cup fresh parsley, finely chopped
- 1 teaspoon ground cumin
- 1 teaspoon ground coriander
- 1/2 teaspoon cayenne pepper (optional, for heat)
- Salt and pepper to taste

For the Pita Dough:

- 3 cups all-purpose flour
- 1 cup warm water
- 2 tablespoons olive oil
- 1 teaspoon sugar
- 1 teaspoon salt
- 1 packet (2 1/4 teaspoons) active dry yeast

For Serving:

- Tahini sauce or garlic sauce
- Pickles or cucumber slices

Instructions:

> Prepare the Meat Filling:
> - In a mixing bowl, combine ground beef or lamb with chopped onion, minced garlic, chopped tomato, fresh parsley, ground cumin, ground coriander, cayenne pepper (if using), salt, and pepper. Mix well to combine.
>
> Make the Pita Dough:

- In a large bowl, combine warm water, sugar, and yeast. Let it sit for about 5 minutes until it becomes frothy. Add olive oil and salt to the yeast mixture. Gradually add the flour, kneading until you have a smooth and elastic dough. Cover the dough and let it rise in a warm place for about 1 hour or until it doubles in size.

Preheat Oven:
- Preheat your oven to the highest temperature it can go (usually around 475°F or 245°C).

Divide and Roll Dough:
- Divide the dough into small balls, roughly the size of a golf ball. On a floured surface, roll each ball into a thin round disk, about 6-8 inches in diameter.

Fill and Seal Pitas:
- Place a portion of the meat filling in the center of each dough round. Fold the edges over the filling and seal the edges, creating a stuffed pita.

Bake:
- Place the stuffed pitas on a baking sheet and bake in the preheated oven for about 10-15 minutes or until the dough is golden and the meat is cooked through.

Serve:
- Serve the hawawshi hot, with tahini sauce or garlic sauce drizzled on top. Add pickles or cucumber slices on the side.

Enjoy:
- Enjoy the delicious and savory hawawshi, a popular Egyptian street food that combines the flavors of spiced meat with freshly baked pita. It's a flavorful and satisfying meal.

Samak Meshwi (Grilled Fish)

Ingredients:

For the Marinade:

- 4 fish fillets (use a firm-fleshed fish like sea bass or tilapia)
- 3 tablespoons olive oil
- Juice of 2 lemons
- 3 cloves garlic, minced
- 1 teaspoon ground cumin
- 1 teaspoon ground coriander
- 1 teaspoon paprika
- Salt and pepper to taste

For Grilling:

- Olive oil for brushing
- Lemon wedges for serving
- Fresh herbs for garnish (such as parsley or cilantro)

Instructions:

Prepare Marinade:
- In a bowl, whisk together olive oil, lemon juice, minced garlic, ground cumin, ground coriander, paprika, salt, and pepper to create the marinade.

Marinate the Fish:
- Place the fish fillets in a shallow dish and pour the marinade over them. Ensure that the fillets are well-coated. Cover the dish and refrigerate for at least 30 minutes to allow the flavors to infuse.

Preheat the Grill:
- Preheat your grill to medium-high heat.

Brush with Olive Oil:
- Brush the grill grates with olive oil to prevent sticking.

Grill the Fish:

- Remove the fish fillets from the marinade and shake off excess. Place the fillets on the preheated grill. Grill each side for about 4-6 minutes, or until the fish is opaque and easily flakes with a fork.

Baste with Marinade:
- During grilling, baste the fish with the remaining marinade to keep it moist and flavorful.

Check for Doneness:
- The fish is done when it reaches an internal temperature of 145°F (63°C) and has a slightly charred appearance.

Serve:
- Transfer the grilled fish to a serving platter. Drizzle with a bit of fresh lemon juice and garnish with chopped fresh herbs.

Garnish and Enjoy:
- Serve the samak meshwi with lemon wedges on the side and additional fresh herbs for garnish. Enjoy this delicious and simple grilled fish dish!

Optional:
- You can also serve the grilled fish with a side of rice, grilled vegetables, or a light salad for a complete meal.

Bamia (Okra Stew)

Ingredients:

- 2 cups fresh okra, trimmed and sliced
- 1 lb lamb or beef stew meat, cubed
- 1 large onion, finely chopped
- 3 cloves garlic, minced
- 1 can (14 oz) diced tomatoes
- 2 tablespoons tomato paste
- 1 teaspoon ground coriander
- 1 teaspoon ground cumin
- 1/2 teaspoon cayenne pepper (optional, for heat)
- Salt and pepper to taste
- 2 tablespoons olive oil
- 4 cups water or beef broth
- Fresh lemon wedges for serving
- Cooked rice for serving

Instructions:

Prepare Okra:
- Trim the tops of the okra and slice them into rounds. If using frozen okra, thaw it before cooking.

Sear Meat:
- In a large pot, heat olive oil over medium-high heat. Add the cubed meat and sear until browned on all sides.

Add Aromatics:
- Add chopped onions to the pot and sauté until they become translucent. Stir in minced garlic and cook until fragrant.

Season Meat:
- Season the meat, onions, and garlic with ground coriander, ground cumin, cayenne pepper (if using), salt, and pepper. Mix well to coat the meat with the spices.

Tomato Base:
- Add diced tomatoes and tomato paste to the pot. Stir to combine the ingredients.

Cook Okra:

- Incorporate the sliced okra into the pot, ensuring it is well-coated with the tomato and spice mixture.

Add Liquid:
- Pour in water or beef broth to the pot. Bring the stew to a boil, then reduce the heat to low and let it simmer. Cover the pot and let it cook until the meat is tender and the okra is cooked through.

Check Seasoning:
- Taste the stew and adjust the seasoning if needed. Add more salt, pepper, or spices according to your preference.

Serve:
- Serve the bamia hot over a bed of cooked rice. Garnish with fresh lemon wedges.

Enjoy:
- Enjoy this hearty and flavorful okra stew as a comforting dish, and squeeze some fresh lemon juice over it for a burst of citrusy flavor. It's a delightful meal that pairs well with rice or bread.

Macarona Bechamel (Egyptian Baked Pasta)

Ingredients:

For the Pasta:

- 1 lb (450g) penne or any pasta shape of your choice
- Water for boiling
- Salt for seasoning

For the Meat Sauce:

- 1 lb (450g) ground beef or a mixture of beef and lamb
- 1 large onion, finely chopped
- 3 cloves garlic, minced
- 1 can (14 oz) crushed tomatoes
- 2 tablespoons tomato paste
- 1 teaspoon ground cinnamon
- 1 teaspoon ground allspice
- Salt and pepper to taste
- 2 tablespoons vegetable oil

For the Bechamel Sauce:

- 4 cups whole milk
- 1/2 cup unsalted butter
- 1/2 cup all-purpose flour
- 1/4 teaspoon ground nutmeg
- Salt and pepper to taste
- 2 large eggs, beaten (for egg wash)

Instructions:

Cook the Pasta:
- Boil the pasta in salted water according to the package instructions until al dente. Drain and set aside.

Prepare Meat Sauce:
- In a large skillet, heat vegetable oil over medium heat. Add chopped onions and sauté until translucent. Add minced garlic and cook until fragrant. Add ground beef (or beef/lamb mixture) and cook until browned.

Stir in crushed tomatoes, tomato paste, ground cinnamon, ground allspice, salt, and pepper. Simmer the meat sauce until it thickens. Set aside.

Make Bechamel Sauce:
- In a saucepan, melt butter over medium heat. Add flour and whisk continuously to create a roux. Gradually add milk while whisking to avoid lumps. Continue whisking until the sauce thickens. Season with ground nutmeg, salt, and pepper.

Assemble Macarona Bechamel:
- Preheat your oven to 350°F (180°C). In a large baking dish, layer half of the cooked pasta, followed by the meat sauce, and then the remaining pasta.

Pour Bechamel Sauce:
- Pour the prepared bechamel sauce over the top, making sure to cover the entire surface.

Brush with Egg Wash:
- Brush the top of the bechamel with beaten eggs to create a golden crust when baked.

Bake:
- Place the baking dish in the preheated oven and bake for approximately 30-40 minutes or until the top is golden brown and the edges are bubbling.

Serve:
- Allow the Macarona Bechamel to cool for a few minutes before serving. Cut into squares or rectangles and serve warm.

Enjoy:
- Enjoy this delicious and comforting Egyptian baked pasta dish, combining layers of pasta, flavorful meat sauce, and a creamy bechamel topping. It's a hearty and satisfying meal.

Kushari Lasagna

Ingredients:

For the Kushari Base:

- 1 cup lentils, rinsed
- 1 cup rice
- 1 cup macaroni
- 1 cup cooked chickpeas (canned or cooked from dry)
- 2 large onions, thinly sliced
- 4 cloves garlic, minced
- 1 can (14 oz) crushed tomatoes
- 2 tablespoons tomato paste
- 2 teaspoons ground cumin
- 1 teaspoon ground coriander
- 1/2 teaspoon cayenne pepper (optional, for heat)
- Salt and pepper to taste
- Vegetable oil for frying onions
- Water for cooking

For the Bechamel Sauce:

- 4 cups whole milk
- 1/2 cup unsalted butter
- 1/2 cup all-purpose flour
- 1/4 teaspoon ground nutmeg
- Salt and pepper to taste
- 2 large eggs, beaten

For Assembly:

- Grated mozzarella cheese
- Grated Parmesan cheese
- Chopped fresh parsley for garnish

Instructions:

Prepare Kushari Base:
- Cook lentils, rice, and macaroni separately according to their package instructions. Set aside.

Make the Tomato Sauce:
- In a saucepan, heat a bit of vegetable oil. Add minced garlic and sauté until fragrant. Add crushed tomatoes, tomato paste, ground cumin, ground coriander, cayenne pepper (if using), salt, and pepper. Simmer for 15-20 minutes until the sauce thickens.

Fry Onions:
- In a separate pan, thinly slice one onion and fry it in vegetable oil until golden brown and crispy. Set aside for garnish.

Prepare Bechamel Sauce:
- In a saucepan, melt butter over medium heat. Add flour and whisk continuously to create a roux. Gradually add milk while whisking to avoid lumps. Continue whisking until the sauce thickens. Season with ground nutmeg, salt, and pepper.

Assemble Kushari Lasagna:
- Preheat your oven to 350°F (180°C). In a deep baking dish, layer the cooked lentils, followed by a layer of rice, then a layer of macaroni, and finally a layer of cooked chickpeas.

Pour Tomato Sauce:
- Pour the prepared tomato sauce over the layers, ensuring it covers the entire surface.

Add Bechamel Sauce:
- Pour the bechamel sauce over the tomato sauce layer. Spread it evenly.

Sprinkle Cheese:
- Sprinkle grated mozzarella and Parmesan cheese over the top.

Repeat Layers:
- Repeat the process, creating another set of layers using the cooked lentils, rice, macaroni, and chickpeas.

Finish with Cheese:
- Pour the remaining tomato sauce and bechamel sauce over the second set of layers. Top with another generous sprinkle of grated mozzarella and Parmesan cheese.

Brush with Beaten Eggs:
- Brush the top with beaten eggs to give it a golden crust when baked.

Bake:
- Place the baking dish in the preheated oven and bake for approximately 30-40 minutes or until the top is golden brown and the edges are bubbling.

Garnish and Serve:
- Garnish with crispy fried onions and chopped fresh parsley.

Enjoy:
- Allow the Kushari Lasagna to cool for a few minutes before serving. Cut into squares and enjoy this unique fusion dish that combines the flavors of Kushari with the comforting layers of lasagna.

Street Food:

Shawarma

Ingredients:

For the Marinade:

- 1.5 to 2 pounds boneless, skinless chicken thighs
- 1 cup plain yogurt
- 4 tablespoons olive oil
- 4 cloves garlic, minced
- 1 teaspoon ground cumin
- 1 teaspoon ground paprika
- 1 teaspoon ground turmeric
- 1 teaspoon ground cinnamon
- 1 teaspoon ground coriander
- 1 teaspoon cayenne pepper (adjust to taste)
- Salt and black pepper to taste
- Juice of 1 lemon

For Garlic Sauce:

- 1 cup mayonnaise
- 4 cloves garlic, minced
- 2 tablespoons fresh lemon juice
- Salt to taste
- Chopped fresh parsley for garnish

For Serving:

- Pita bread or flatbreads
- Sliced tomatoes
- Sliced cucumbers
- Sliced red onions
- Pickles

Instructions:

Marinate the Chicken:
- In a bowl, combine all the marinade ingredients. Add the chicken thighs to the marinade, making sure they are well-coated. Cover and refrigerate for at least 2 hours or overnight for best results.

Preheat Oven or Grill:
- Preheat your oven to 400°F (200°C) or heat a grill to medium-high.

Cook the Chicken:
- If using an oven, place the marinated chicken on a baking sheet and roast for 25-30 minutes or until fully cooked, turning halfway through. If using a grill, cook the chicken for about 5-7 minutes per side or until fully cooked. The chicken should have a nice char on the edges.

Make Garlic Sauce:
- While the chicken is cooking, prepare the garlic sauce. In a bowl, mix together mayonnaise, minced garlic, fresh lemon juice, and salt. Adjust the seasoning to your taste. Refrigerate until ready to serve.

Rest and Slice:
- Let the cooked chicken rest for a few minutes before slicing it thinly.

Prepare the Shawarma:
- Heat the pita bread or flatbreads. Place sliced shawarma chicken on the bread.

Assemble:
- Add sliced tomatoes, cucumbers, red onions, and pickles to the shawarma. Drizzle with garlic sauce.

Garnish and Serve:
- Garnish with chopped fresh parsley and serve the chicken shawarma immediately.

Enjoy:
- Enjoy the delicious homemade chicken shawarma with all the fixings. It's a flavorful and satisfying dish that captures the essence of Middle Eastern street food.

Hawawshi (Meat Pie)

Ingredients:

For the Dough:

- 3 cups all-purpose flour
- 1 teaspoon active dry yeast
- 1 teaspoon sugar
- 1 teaspoon salt
- 1 cup warm water

For the Filling:

- 1 lb ground beef or lamb
- 1 large onion, finely chopped
- 2 tomatoes, finely chopped
- 1/4 cup fresh parsley, chopped
- 2 cloves garlic, minced
- 1 teaspoon ground cumin
- 1 teaspoon ground coriander
- 1 teaspoon paprika
- Salt and pepper to taste

For Assembling:

- Olive oil for brushing

Instructions:

Prepare Dough:
- In a bowl, mix warm water, sugar, and active dry yeast. Allow it to sit for 5-10 minutes until frothy. In a large mixing bowl, combine flour and salt. Add the yeast mixture, and knead until you have a smooth and elastic dough. Cover and let it rise in a warm place for about 1 hour, or until doubled in size.

Make Filling:
- In a skillet, cook ground beef or lamb over medium heat until browned. Drain excess fat. Add chopped onions, tomatoes, parsley, minced garlic,

ground cumin, ground coriander, paprika, salt, and pepper. Cook until the vegetables are softened and the mixture is well combined. Set aside.

Preheat Oven:
- Preheat your oven to 400°F (200°C).

Divide Dough:
- Divide the risen dough into equal portions, shaping them into balls.

Roll Out Dough:
- On a floured surface, roll out each ball of dough into a thin, flat round shape.

Add Filling:
- Place a portion of the meat filling in the center of each dough round, leaving some space around the edges.

Fold and Seal:
- Fold the dough over the filling, creating a half-moon shape. Press the edges to seal the pie.

Brush with Olive Oil:
- Place the sealed pies on a baking sheet. Brush the tops with olive oil.

Bake:
- Bake in the preheated oven for about 20-25 minutes or until the pies are golden brown and cooked through.

Serve:
- Serve the hawawshi pies warm. They can be enjoyed as is or with your favorite dipping sauce.

Enjoy:
- Enjoy the delicious hawawshi, a flavorful and savory meat pie that originated from Egyptian cuisine. It's a delightful handheld meal that combines a crisp crust with a spiced meat filling.

Tameya Sandwich (Falafel Sandwich)

Ingredients:

For the Falafel:

- 2 cups dried chickpeas
- 1 small onion, roughly chopped
- 3 cloves garlic, minced
- 1 cup fresh parsley, chopped
- 1 cup fresh cilantro, chopped
- 1 teaspoon ground cumin
- 1 teaspoon ground coriander
- 1/2 teaspoon cayenne pepper (optional, for heat)
- Salt and pepper to taste
- 1 teaspoon baking soda
- 4 tablespoons all-purpose flour
- Vegetable oil for frying

For the Tahini Sauce:

- 1/2 cup tahini
- 2 tablespoons fresh lemon juice
- 2 tablespoons water
- 1 clove garlic, minced
- Salt to taste

For the Sandwich:

- Pita bread or flatbreads
- Sliced tomatoes
- Sliced cucumbers
- Shredded lettuce
- Pickles (optional)
- Thinly sliced red onions
- Hot sauce (optional)

Instructions:

Prepare Chickpeas:
- Soak dried chickpeas in water overnight. Drain and rinse.

Make Falafel Mixture:
- In a food processor, combine soaked chickpeas, chopped onion, minced garlic, fresh parsley, fresh cilantro, ground cumin, ground coriander, cayenne pepper (if using), salt, and pepper. Pulse until the mixture is coarse.

Add Baking Soda and Flour:
- Add baking soda and all-purpose flour to the mixture. Pulse until everything is well combined. The mixture should be slightly coarse, not a smooth paste.

Chill the Mixture:
- Refrigerate the falafel mixture for at least 1 hour. This helps the mixture firm up and makes it easier to handle.

Shape Falafel:
- Scoop portions of the chilled falafel mixture and shape them into small patties or balls.

Fry Falafel:
- In a deep pan, heat vegetable oil to 350°F (180°C). Carefully fry the falafel until they are golden brown and crispy. Remove and place on a paper towel to absorb excess oil.

Make Tahini Sauce:
- In a bowl, whisk together tahini, fresh lemon juice, water, minced garlic, and salt to make the tahini sauce. Adjust the consistency by adding more water if needed.

Assemble the Sandwich:
- Warm the pita bread or flatbreads. Place falafel inside, and add sliced tomatoes, cucumbers, shredded lettuce, pickles (if using), and thinly sliced red onions.

Drizzle with Tahini Sauce:
- Drizzle the tahini sauce over the sandwich. Add hot sauce if you like it spicy.

Serve:
- Serve the Tameya Sandwich immediately while the falafel is still warm.

Enjoy:

- Enjoy this classic Tameya Sandwich, a delicious and satisfying street food that brings together the crispy goodness of falafel with fresh and flavorful toppings.

Baladi Bread with Cheese and Herbs

Ingredients:

- Baladi bread (or any flatbread of your choice)
- Feta cheese, crumbled
- Fresh herbs (such as parsley, mint, or cilantro), chopped
- Olive oil
- Cherry tomatoes, sliced (optional)
- Black olives, pitted and sliced (optional)
- Salt and pepper to taste

Instructions:

Prepare the Baladi Bread:
- If the baladi bread is not fresh, you can warm it up by briefly placing it on a hot griddle or in the oven. Warm it until it becomes pliable but not crispy.

Spread Feta Cheese:
- Crumble the feta cheese and spread it over the warm baladi bread.

Add Fresh Herbs:
- Sprinkle the chopped fresh herbs over the feta cheese. Use a combination of parsley, mint, cilantro, or any herbs you prefer.

Optional Toppings:
- If desired, add sliced cherry tomatoes and black olives on top of the herbs and cheese for extra flavor and freshness.

Drizzle with Olive Oil:
- Drizzle olive oil over the entire bread, ensuring that the cheese and herbs are well-coated.

Season with Salt and Pepper:
- Season the bread with a pinch of salt and a sprinkle of black pepper according to your taste.

Serve:
- Serve the baladi bread with cheese and herbs immediately while it's still warm and the flavors are vibrant.

Enjoy:
- Enjoy this simple and delightful Baladi Bread with Cheese and Herbs as a quick snack or appetizer. The combination of creamy feta, fresh herbs, and the warmth of the bread creates a delicious and satisfying bite.

Side Dishes:

Egyptian Pickles

Ingredients:

For the Pickling Solution:

- 4 cups water
- 1 cup white vinegar
- 2 tablespoons salt
- 1 tablespoon sugar

For the Vegetables:

- Cucumbers, washed and quartered (small pickling cucumbers work well)
- Carrots, peeled and cut into sticks
- Cauliflower florets
- Garlic cloves, peeled
- Fresh dill (optional)
- Whole black peppercorns
- Bay leaves (optional)
- Grape leaves (optional)

Instructions:

Prepare the Pickling Solution:
- In a saucepan, combine water, white vinegar, salt, and sugar. Bring the mixture to a boil, stirring until the salt and sugar are fully dissolved. Remove from heat and let the pickling solution cool to room temperature.

Prepare the Vegetables:
- Wash and prepare the vegetables you want to pickle. Cut cucumbers into quarters, peel and cut carrots into sticks, and separate cauliflower into florets. If using large garlic cloves, you can leave them whole, or slice them if preferred.

Assemble Jars:
- Sterilize glass jars by boiling them in water for a few minutes or running them through the dishwasher. Allow the jars to cool completely.

Layer Vegetables in Jars:

- In each sterilized jar, layer the vegetables along with fresh dill, black peppercorns, and any optional ingredients like bay leaves or grape leaves.

Pour Pickling Solution:
- Pour the cooled pickling solution into each jar, ensuring that the vegetables are fully submerged. Leave a little space at the top of the jar.

Seal Jars:
- Seal the jars tightly with lids.

Store in Refrigerator:
- Place the jars in the refrigerator. The pickles will start to develop flavor after a day or two, but they can be enjoyed even after a few hours.

Allow Pickling Time:
- Allow the pickles to sit in the refrigerator for at least a week to develop their full flavor. The longer they sit, the more flavorful they will become.

Serve:
- Once the pickles have reached your desired level of flavor, serve them as a refreshing and tangy accompaniment to meals or as a crunchy snack.

Enjoy:
- Enjoy these homemade Egyptian pickles with their unique blend of flavors. They make a delicious and traditional addition to many Middle Eastern dishes.

Torshi (Pickled Vegetables)

Ingredients:

For the Pickling Solution:

- 4 cups water
- 2 cups white vinegar
- 2 tablespoons salt
- 2 tablespoons sugar

For the Vegetables:

- Mixed vegetables of your choice (carrots, cauliflower, cucumbers, turnips, bell peppers, etc.)
- Garlic cloves, peeled
- Fresh herbs (dill, mint, parsley, etc.)
- Whole black peppercorns
- Mustard seeds (optional)
- Red pepper flakes (optional)

Instructions:

Prepare the Pickling Solution:
- In a large saucepan, combine water, white vinegar, salt, and sugar. Bring the mixture to a boil, stirring until the salt and sugar are fully dissolved. Remove from heat and let the pickling solution cool to room temperature.

Prepare the Vegetables:
- Wash and prepare the vegetables you want to pickle. Cut them into bite-sized pieces or shapes of your choice.

Assemble Jars:
- Sterilize glass jars by boiling them in water for a few minutes or running them through the dishwasher. Allow the jars to cool completely.

Layer Vegetables in Jars:
- In each sterilized jar, layer the mixed vegetables, garlic cloves, fresh herbs, black peppercorns, and any optional ingredients like mustard seeds or red pepper flakes.

Pour Pickling Solution:
- Pour the cooled pickling solution into each jar, ensuring that the vegetables are fully submerged. Leave a little space at the top of the jar.

Seal Jars:
- Seal the jars tightly with lids.

Store in a Cool Place:
- Place the jars in a cool, dark place for the pickling process to take place. This can be a pantry or cupboard.

Wait for Pickling:
- Allow the torshi to pickle for at least 2-3 weeks, or longer for more intense flavors. Shake the jars gently every few days to ensure even pickling.

Refrigerate After Opening:
- Once you open a jar of torshi, store it in the refrigerator to extend its shelf life.

Serve:
- Serve the torshi as a side dish or condiment. It pairs well with various Middle Eastern dishes, grilled meats, or as a tangy addition to salads.

Enjoy:
- Enjoy the complex and flavorful torshi as a delightful addition to your meals. These pickled vegetables offer a burst of tanginess and crunch to your culinary creations.

Egyptian Lentil Soup

Ingredients:

- 1 cup dried red lentils, rinsed and drained
- 1 large onion, finely chopped
- 3 cloves garlic, minced
- 1 large carrot, peeled and diced
- 1 celery stalk, diced
- 1 medium potato, peeled and diced
- 1 can (14 oz) diced tomatoes
- 1 teaspoon ground cumin
- 1 teaspoon ground coriander
- 1/2 teaspoon turmeric
- 1/4 teaspoon cayenne pepper (optional, for heat)
- 6 cups vegetable or chicken broth
- 2 tablespoons olive oil
- Salt and pepper to taste
- Fresh lemon wedges for serving
- Chopped fresh parsley for garnish

Instructions:

Sauté Aromatics:
- In a large pot, heat olive oil over medium heat. Add chopped onions and sauté until they become translucent. Add minced garlic and cook until fragrant.

Add Vegetables:
- Add diced carrots, celery, and potatoes to the pot. Cook for a few minutes until the vegetables start to soften.

Add Lentils and Spices:
- Add rinsed red lentils to the pot. Stir in ground cumin, ground coriander, turmeric, and cayenne pepper (if using). Mix well to coat the vegetables and lentils with the spices.

Pour in Broth:
- Pour in the vegetable or chicken broth, and add the diced tomatoes. Bring the soup to a boil.

Simmer:

- Reduce the heat to low, cover the pot, and let the soup simmer for about 20-25 minutes or until the lentils and vegetables are tender.

Season:
- Season the soup with salt and pepper according to your taste. Adjust the spices if needed.

Blend (Optional):
- For a smoother consistency, you can use an immersion blender to partially blend the soup. This step is optional, and you can leave the soup chunky if you prefer.

Serve:
- Ladle the Egyptian lentil soup into bowls. Squeeze fresh lemon juice over each serving.

Garnish:
- Garnish the soup with chopped fresh parsley.

Enjoy:
- Enjoy this comforting and nutritious Egyptian lentil soup on its own or with a slice of crusty bread. It's a wholesome dish with a perfect blend of flavors.

Dukkah (Nut and Spice Blend)

Ingredients:

- 1/2 cup hazelnuts
- 1/4 cup sesame seeds
- 2 tablespoons coriander seeds
- 1 tablespoon cumin seeds
- 1 tablespoon black peppercorns
- 1/2 teaspoon sea salt (adjust to taste)
- Optional: 1 teaspoon fennel seeds, 1 teaspoon dried thyme, or 1 teaspoon dried mint for additional flavor

Instructions:

Toast Nuts and Seeds:
- In a dry skillet over medium heat, toast the hazelnuts, sesame seeds, coriander seeds, cumin seeds, and black peppercorns. Stir frequently to prevent burning. Toast until the nuts are fragrant and the seeds are golden brown. This usually takes about 5-7 minutes.

Cool:
- Allow the toasted nuts and seeds to cool completely before proceeding to the next step.

Grind:
- In a food processor or spice grinder, combine the toasted hazelnuts, sesame seeds, coriander seeds, cumin seeds, black peppercorns, and salt. Pulse until the mixture has a coarse, crumbly texture. Be careful not to over-process; you want a bit of texture remaining.

Optional Additions:
- If desired, add fennel seeds, dried thyme, or dried mint to the mixture and pulse a few times to combine.

Adjust Seasoning:
- Taste the dukkah and adjust the salt or other seasonings according to your preference.

Store:
- Transfer the dukkah to an airtight container and store it in a cool, dark place. It can be kept for several weeks.

Serve:

- Dukkah is versatile and can be used in various ways. Serve it as a dip with bread and olive oil, sprinkle it over salads, use it as a coating for meats or fish, or simply enjoy it as a seasoning for a variety of dishes.

Enjoy:

- Enjoy the rich and aromatic flavors of homemade dukkah as it adds depth and crunch to your favorite dishes.

Desserts:

Basbousa (Semolina Cake)

Ingredients:

For the Cake:

- 1 cup semolina
- 1 cup plain yogurt
- 1 cup granulated sugar
- 1 cup desiccated coconut
- 1/2 cup unsalted butter, melted
- 1 teaspoon baking powder
- 1/4 teaspoon baking soda
- 1/4 teaspoon salt
- 1 teaspoon vanilla extract
- Blanched almonds or pine nuts for garnish (optional)

For the Sugar Syrup:

- 1 cup granulated sugar
- 1/2 cup water
- 1 teaspoon lemon juice
- 1 teaspoon rose water or orange blossom water (optional)

Instructions:

Preheat Oven:
- Preheat your oven to 350°F (175°C). Grease a baking dish or cake pan with butter or oil.

Prepare the Cake Batter:
- In a mixing bowl, combine semolina, yogurt, sugar, desiccated coconut, melted butter, baking powder, baking soda, salt, and vanilla extract. Mix well until all the ingredients are thoroughly combined.

Rest the Batter:
- Let the batter rest for about 10-15 minutes. This allows the semolina to absorb the liquid.

Pour into Pan:

- Pour the batter into the greased baking dish, smoothing the top with a spatula.

Bake:
- Bake in the preheated oven for approximately 30-40 minutes or until the top is golden brown and a toothpick inserted into the center comes out clean.

Prepare Sugar Syrup:
- While the cake is baking, prepare the sugar syrup. In a saucepan, combine sugar, water, and lemon juice. Bring to a boil, then reduce the heat and simmer for about 10 minutes. Add rose water or orange blossom water if using. Remove from heat and let it cool.

Cool and Cut:
- Once the cake is baked, allow it to cool for a few minutes. While it's still warm, cut the cake into diamond or square shapes.

Pour Sugar Syrup:
- Pour the cooled sugar syrup over the warm cake, ensuring that it soaks in evenly. Let the cake absorb the syrup for at least 1-2 hours before serving.

Garnish (Optional):
- If desired, garnish each piece with blanched almonds or pine nuts.

Serve:
- Serve the basbousa at room temperature. It's traditionally enjoyed with a cup of tea or coffee.

Enjoy:
- Enjoy this moist and flavorful semolina cake with the perfect balance of sweetness and the aromatic touch of rose water or orange blossom water.

Umm Ali (Bread Pudding)

Ingredients:

- 4 to 5 sheets of puff pastry or 6 to 8 croissants, torn into pieces
- 4 cups whole milk
- 1 cup heavy cream
- 1 cup sugar
- 1/2 cup unsweetened shredded coconut
- 1/2 cup chopped nuts (almonds, pistachios, or hazelnuts)
- 1/4 cup raisins or sultanas
- 1 teaspoon vanilla extract
- Pinch of ground cinnamon
- Pinch of ground nutmeg
- Pinch of salt
- Whipped cream for topping (optional)

Instructions:

Preheat Oven:
- Preheat your oven to 375°F (190°C).

Prepare Puff Pastry or Croissants:
- If using puff pastry sheets, bake them according to the package instructions until they are golden brown and puffed. If using croissants, you can tear them into pieces without baking.

Layer in Baking Dish:
- In a baking dish, layer the baked puff pastry or torn croissants.

Prepare Milk Mixture:
- In a saucepan, heat the whole milk, heavy cream, and sugar over medium heat. Stir until the sugar is dissolved, and the mixture is warm. Do not boil.

Add Flavorings:
- Stir in the vanilla extract, shredded coconut, chopped nuts, raisins or sultanas, ground cinnamon, ground nutmeg, and a pinch of salt.

Pour over Pastry:
- Pour the milk mixture over the layered puff pastry or croissants in the baking dish, ensuring that the pieces are well-soaked.

Bake:

- Bake in the preheated oven for about 25-30 minutes or until the top is golden brown and the mixture is set.

Serve Warm:
- Remove from the oven and let it cool slightly before serving.

Optional Toppings:
- Top with whipped cream if desired. Some variations include a sprinkle of additional nuts or a dusting of powdered sugar.

Serve:
- Serve Umm Ali warm. It's traditionally enjoyed as a dessert or sweet treat.

Enjoy:
- Enjoy the rich and comforting flavors of Umm Ali, a classic Egyptian bread pudding that combines the goodness of puff pastry or croissants with a creamy, spiced milk mixture.

Roz Bel Laban w Nataf (Rice Pudding with Coconut)

Ingredients:

- 1 cup short-grain rice
- 4 cups whole milk
- 1 cup coconut milk
- 1 cup granulated sugar (adjust to taste)
- 1/2 cup desiccated coconut
- 1/2 teaspoon vanilla extract
- Pinch of salt
- Ground cinnamon for garnish (optional)

Instructions:

Rinse the Rice:
- Rinse the short-grain rice under cold water until the water runs clear. This helps remove excess starch.

Cook the Rice:
- In a large saucepan, combine the rinsed rice, whole milk, and coconut milk. Bring to a gentle boil over medium heat, then reduce the heat to low and simmer. Stir occasionally to prevent sticking.

Add Sugar and Coconut:
- Once the rice is partially cooked and the mixture has thickened, add granulated sugar, desiccated coconut, vanilla extract, and a pinch of salt. Continue to simmer and stir until the rice is fully cooked and the pudding reaches a creamy consistency.

Adjust Sweetness:
- Taste the pudding and adjust the sweetness by adding more sugar if needed. Keep in mind that the sweetness will intensify as the pudding cools.

Remove from Heat:
- Once the rice pudding has reached the desired consistency, remove it from heat.

Serve Warm or Chilled:
- You can serve Roz Bel Laban w Nataf warm directly from the stove, or let it cool and refrigerate for a few hours until chilled.

Garnish (Optional):

- If desired, sprinkle ground cinnamon on top before serving for an extra layer of flavor.

Serve:
- Spoon the rice pudding into individual bowls or dishes.

Enjoy:
- Enjoy the delightful combination of rice and coconut in this Roz Bel Laban w Nataf. It's a comforting and sweet treat that can be served as a dessert or enjoyed as a snack.

Qatayef (Stuffed Pancakes)

Ingredients:

For the Qatayef:

- 2 cups all-purpose flour
- 1 teaspoon baking powder
- 1 tablespoon sugar
- 1 1/2 cups lukewarm water
- 1 teaspoon active dry yeast
- Pinch of salt
- 1/2 teaspoon baking soda

For the Cream Filling:

- 2 cups ricotta cheese
- 1/2 cup sugar
- 1 tablespoon orange blossom water (optional)
- Chopped pistachios for garnish (optional)

For the Nut Filling:

- 1 cup mixed nuts (walnuts, pistachios, almonds), finely chopped
- 1/4 cup sugar
- 1/2 teaspoon ground cinnamon
- Orange blossom water (optional)

For the Sugar Syrup:

- 1 cup sugar
- 1/2 cup water
- 1 teaspoon lemon juice
- 1 teaspoon rose water or orange blossom water (optional)

Instructions:

1. Prepare the Qatayef Batter:

    - In a bowl, mix the lukewarm water, sugar, and yeast. Let it sit for about 5-10 minutes until frothy.
    - In a large mixing bowl, combine the flour, baking powder, and a pinch of salt. Pour the yeast mixture into the dry ingredients and mix well. Let the batter rest for 30 minutes to an hour, allowing it to rise.
    - Just before cooking, add the baking soda to the batter and mix gently.

2. Make the Cream Filling:

    - In a bowl, mix the ricotta cheese, sugar, and orange blossom water until well combined. Set aside.

3. Make the Nut Filling:

    - In a separate bowl, mix the chopped nuts, sugar, and ground cinnamon. Add a little orange blossom water if desired. Set aside.

4. Cook the Qatayef:

    - Heat a non-stick skillet or griddle over medium-low heat. Pour small rounds of batter onto the skillet to form small pancakes (about 2 inches in diameter).
    - Cook only on one side until bubbles form and the surface looks set. The Qatayef should be thin and not flipped to cook the other side.

5. Fill the Qatayef:

    - As the Qatayef cook, remove them from the skillet and place them on a clean kitchen towel. Place a spoonful of the cream or nut filling in the center of each pancake, then fold it in half to form a half-moon shape.

6. Seal the Edges:

    - Pinch the edges of the Qatayef to seal them, creating a stuffed pouch.

7. Prepare Sugar Syrup:

- In a saucepan, combine sugar, water, and lemon juice. Bring to a boil, then reduce heat and simmer for about 10 minutes until it thickens slightly. Add rose water or orange blossom water if desired. Let the sugar syrup cool.

8. Serve:

- Arrange the stuffed Qatayef on a serving platter and drizzle the sugar syrup over them. Garnish with chopped pistachios if desired.

9. Enjoy:

- Qatayef is best enjoyed fresh and warm. Serve these delightful stuffed pancakes as a delicious dessert during special occasions or celebrations.

Kunafa (Middle Eastern Pastry)

Ingredients:

For the Kunafa Dough:

- 1 pound (about 450g) kataifi dough (shredded phyllo dough)
- 1 cup unsalted butter, melted

For the Cheese Filling:

- 2 cups shredded mozzarella cheese
- 1 cup ricotta cheese or unsalted akkawi cheese (traditional choice)
- 1/4 cup sugar
- 1 teaspoon orange blossom water or rose water (optional)

For the Sugar Syrup:

- 1 cup sugar
- 1/2 cup water
- 1 teaspoon lemon juice
- 1 teaspoon orange blossom water or rose water (optional)

For Garnish (Optional):

- Chopped pistachios or slivered almonds

Instructions:

1. Prepare the Sugar Syrup:

- In a saucepan, combine sugar, water, and lemon juice. Bring to a boil, then reduce heat and simmer for about 10 minutes until it thickens slightly. Add orange blossom water or rose water if desired. Let the sugar syrup cool.

2. Make the Cheese Filling:

- In a bowl, combine shredded mozzarella cheese, ricotta or akkawi cheese, sugar, and orange blossom water. Mix well until the ingredients are evenly distributed.

3. Prepare the Kunafa Dough:

- Preheat your oven to 350°F (175°C).
- Separate the kataifi dough strands with your hands. Pour the melted butter over the dough and toss it gently to coat the strands evenly.

4. Assemble the Kunafa:

- Take half of the buttered kataifi dough and press it into the bottom of a round or square baking dish to form a crust.
- Spread the cheese filling evenly over the dough layer.
- Cover the cheese filling with the remaining half of the buttered kataifi dough, pressing it down gently.

5. Bake:

- Bake in the preheated oven for about 30-40 minutes or until the kunafa is golden brown and crispy.

6. Cut and Pour Sugar Syrup:

- While the kunafa is still hot, cut it into squares or diamond shapes. Pour the cooled sugar syrup over the hot kunafa, allowing it to soak in.

7. Garnish (Optional):

- Garnish the kunafa with chopped pistachios or slivered almonds if desired.

8. Serve:

- Allow the kunafa to cool slightly before serving. It can be enjoyed warm or at room temperature.

9. Enjoy:

- Kunafa is a delightful Middle Eastern pastry that combines the crunchiness of shredded phyllo dough with a sweet and cheesy filling. Serve it as a dessert on special occasions or celebrations.

Aish El Saraya (Bread Pudding with Custard)

Ingredients:

For the Bread Pudding:

- 8 slices of white bread, crusts removed
- 1/2 cup unsalted butter, melted
- 1 cup sugar
- 1 cup water
- 1 tablespoon orange blossom water or rose water (optional)

For the Custard:

- 4 cups whole milk
- 1 cup sugar
- 1/2 cup cornstarch
- 4 egg yolks
- 1 teaspoon vanilla extract

For Garnish:

- Chopped pistachios or almonds
- Ground cinnamon (optional)

Instructions:

1. Prepare the Bread Pudding:

- Preheat your oven to 350°F (175°C).
- Brush each slice of bread with melted butter on both sides. Arrange the bread slices in a single layer in a baking dish.
- In a saucepan, combine sugar and water over medium heat. Stir until the sugar dissolves and the mixture comes to a boil. Remove from heat and add orange blossom water or rose water if using.
- Pour the sugar syrup evenly over the arranged bread slices, ensuring they are well-soaked.

2. Make the Custard:

- In a bowl, whisk together egg yolks, sugar, and cornstarch until well combined.
- In a saucepan, heat the milk over medium heat until it's warm but not boiling. Slowly pour the warm milk into the egg yolk mixture while whisking continuously to avoid curdling.
- Pour the mixture back into the saucepan and cook over medium heat, stirring constantly until the custard thickens. Remove from heat and stir in the vanilla extract.

3. Assemble and Bake:

- Pour the custard over the soaked bread slices in the baking dish.
- Bake in the preheated oven for about 20-25 minutes or until the custard is set and the top is golden brown.

4. Garnish:

- Once out of the oven, sprinkle chopped pistachios or almonds over the top. Optionally, dust with ground cinnamon for extra flavor.

5. Serve:

- Allow Aish El Saraya to cool slightly before serving. It can be enjoyed warm or at room temperature.

6. Enjoy:

- Aish El Saraya is a delicious bread pudding with a rich custard layer, perfect for satisfying your sweet cravings. Serve it as a dessert on special occasions or family gatherings.

Ghorayeba (Butter Cookies)

Ingredients:

- 1 cup unsalted butter, softened
- 1 cup powdered sugar
- 2 cups all-purpose flour
- 1/4 cup cornstarch
- 1/4 teaspoon baking powder
- 1/4 teaspoon salt
- 1 teaspoon vanilla extract
- Chopped pistachios or whole almonds for garnish (optional)

Instructions:

1. Preheat Oven:

- Preheat your oven to 350°F (175°C). Line a baking sheet with parchment paper.

2. Cream Butter and Sugar:

- In a large bowl, cream together the softened butter and powdered sugar until light and fluffy.

3. Sift Dry Ingredients:

- In a separate bowl, sift together the all-purpose flour, cornstarch, baking powder, and salt.

4. Combine and Add Vanilla:

- Gradually add the sifted dry ingredients to the butter and sugar mixture, mixing until well combined. Stir in the vanilla extract.

5. Shape Cookies:

- Take small portions of the dough and shape them into small balls or crescent shapes. Place the cookies on the prepared baking sheet, leaving a little space between each.

6. Garnish (Optional):

- If desired, press a chopped pistachio or a whole almond into the center of each cookie for garnish.

7. Bake:

- Bake in the preheated oven for about 12-15 minutes or until the edges are lightly golden.

8. Cool:

- Allow the Ghorayeba cookies to cool on the baking sheet for a few minutes before transferring them to a wire rack to cool completely.

9. Store:

- Once completely cooled, store the butter cookies in an airtight container.

10. Enjoy:

- Enjoy these delicate and melt-in-your-mouth Ghorayeba cookies with a cup of tea or coffee. They are perfect for festive occasions or as a sweet treat anytime.

Beverages:

Hibiscus Tea (Karkadeh)

Ingredients:

- 1 cup dried hibiscus petals (karkadeh)
- 4 cups water
- 1/2 to 3/4 cup sugar (adjust to taste)
- 1 cinnamon stick (optional)
- 1-2 slices of fresh ginger (optional)
- 1 teaspoon orange blossom water or rose water (optional)
- Ice cubes (for serving)
- Orange slices or mint leaves for garnish (optional)

Instructions:

1. Rinse the Hibiscus Petals:

- Rinse the dried hibiscus petals under cold water to remove any impurities.

2. Boil Water:

- In a pot, bring 4 cups of water to a boil.

3. Add Hibiscus Petals:

- Once the water is boiling, add the rinsed hibiscus petals to the pot.

4. Simmer:

- Reduce the heat to low and let the hibiscus petals simmer for about 10-15 minutes. The water will turn deep red as it absorbs the flavor and color from the petals.

5. Add Sweetener:

- Add sugar to the pot and stir until it dissolves. You can adjust the amount of sugar based on your preference for sweetness.

6. Add Optional Ingredients:

- If desired, add a cinnamon stick and slices of fresh ginger to the pot for added flavor. Allow them to simmer with the hibiscus petals.

7. Strain:

- After simmering, remove the pot from heat and strain the hibiscus tea to remove the petals and any additional ingredients.

8. Cool:

- Allow the tea to cool to room temperature. You can also refrigerate it for a refreshing iced tea later.

9. Add Optional Flavors:

If you like, you can add a teaspoon of orange blossom water or rose water to enhance the flavor of the hibiscus tea.

10. Serve:

- Pour the hibiscus tea over ice cubes in glasses.

11. Garnish (Optional):

- Garnish the hibiscus tea with orange slices or mint leaves for a decorative touch.

12. Enjoy:

- Enjoy your homemade hibiscus tea (Karkadeh)! It's a refreshing and vibrant beverage that can be served hot or cold, making it perfect for any occasion.

Sahlab (Warm Milk Pudding)

Ingredients:

- 4 cups whole milk
- 1/4 cup cornstarch
- 1/2 cup sugar (adjust to taste)
- 2 tablespoons sahlab powder
- 1 teaspoon rose water or orange blossom water
- Ground cinnamon for garnish
- Chopped nuts (such as pistachios or almonds) for garnish

Instructions:

1. Dissolve Sahlab Powder:

- In a small bowl, dissolve the sahlab powder in a couple of tablespoons of cold milk. Make sure it forms a smooth paste.

2. Mix Cornstarch:

- In a separate bowl, mix the cornstarch with a small amount of cold milk to create a smooth slurry.

3. Heat Milk:

- In a saucepan, heat the remaining milk over medium heat until it's warm but not boiling.

4. Add Sugar:

- Add sugar to the warm milk and stir until it dissolves.

5. Add Sahlab Mixture:

- Pour the sahlab powder mixture into the warm milk, stirring continuously to prevent lumps from forming.

6. Add Cornstarch Mixture:

- Pour the cornstarch slurry into the milk and continue to stir.

7. Thicken the Pudding:

    - Keep stirring the mixture over medium heat until it thickens. This might take about 10-15 minutes. The pudding should have a creamy consistency.

8. Add Flavoring:

    - Stir in the rose water or orange blossom water for a fragrant touch.

9. Serve:

    - Once the Sahlab pudding reaches the desired thickness, remove it from heat.

10. Pour into Cups:

    - Pour the warm Sahlab pudding into individual serving cups.

11. Garnish:

    - Garnish the Sahlab with a sprinkle of ground cinnamon and chopped nuts.

12. Enjoy:

    - Serve Sahlab warm and enjoy this comforting milk pudding with its unique flavor and creamy texture. It's a delightful treat, especially during colder months.

Sobia (Coconut Drink)

Ingredients:

- 1 cup rice
- 4 cups water
- 4 cups coconut milk
- 1 cup sugar (adjust to taste)
- 1 teaspoon vanilla extract
- 1 cup shredded coconut (optional, for texture)
- Ice cubes (for serving)

Instructions:

1. Rinse and Soak Rice:

- Rinse the rice under cold water. In a bowl, soak the rice in water for at least 2 hours or overnight.

2. Blend Rice:

- Drain the soaked rice and blend it with 2 cups of water until you get a smooth mixture.

3. Strain Rice Mixture:

- Strain the blended rice mixture through a fine sieve or cheesecloth, extracting the rice milk. Discard the rice solids.

4. Mix with Coconut Milk:

- In a large pot, combine the extracted rice milk, coconut milk, and sugar. Stir well to dissolve the sugar.

5. Heat Mixture:

- Place the pot over medium heat and bring the mixture to a gentle simmer. Stir occasionally to prevent sticking.

6. Add Vanilla Extract:

- Once the mixture is simmering, add vanilla extract and continue to simmer for about 15-20 minutes. Stir occasionally.

7. Cool:

- Allow the Sobia mixture to cool to room temperature.

8. Optional: Add Shredded Coconut:

- If you prefer a textured drink, you can add shredded coconut to the cooled Sobia mixture.

9. Chill:

- Refrigerate the Sobia until it's well chilled.

10. Serve:

- Serve Sobia over ice cubes in glasses.

11. Enjoy:

- Enjoy the refreshing and creamy flavor of Sobia, a coconut and rice drink that is perfect for cooling down on a hot day.

Tamarind Juice (Tamr Hindi)

Ingredients:

- 1 cup tamarind pulp
- 4 cups water
- 1 cup sugar (adjust to taste)
- 1/2 teaspoon salt
- Ice cubes (for serving)
- Fresh mint leaves for garnish (optional)

Instructions:

1. Prepare Tamarind Pulp:

- Soak the tamarind pulp in 2 cups of warm water for about 30 minutes. Mash the tamarind to extract its flavor.

2. Strain Tamarind Mixture:

- Strain the soaked tamarind through a fine sieve or cheesecloth, extracting the tamarind juice. Discard any solids.

3. Mix Sugar and Salt:

- In a pitcher, combine the tamarind juice with the remaining 2 cups of water. Add sugar and salt to the mixture. Stir well until the sugar dissolves.

4. Adjust Sweetness:

- Taste the tamarind juice and adjust the sweetness by adding more sugar if needed.

5. Chill:

- Refrigerate the tamarind juice until it's well chilled.

6. Serve:

- Pour the chilled tamarind juice over ice cubes in glasses.

7. Garnish (Optional):

- Garnish with fresh mint leaves for an extra burst of flavor and aroma.

8. Enjoy:

- Enjoy the tangy and refreshing taste of Tamarind Juice (Tamr Hindi). It's a popular and cooling beverage, especially during hot weather.

Qamar al-Din (Apricot Juice)

Ingredients:

- 1 cup dried apricot sheets (Qamar al-Din)
- 4 cups water
- 1/2 to 3/4 cup sugar (adjust to taste)
- 1 tablespoon orange blossom water (optional)
- Ice cubes (for serving)

Instructions:

1. Soak Apricot Sheets:

- Begin by soaking the dried apricot sheets (Qamar al-Din) in warm water for several hours or overnight. Ensure they are fully submerged and softened.

2. Blend Apricot Sheets:

- After soaking, blend the softened apricot sheets with the water until you get a smooth apricot puree.

3. Strain Mixture:

- Strain the blended apricot mixture through a fine sieve or cheesecloth to remove any solids, obtaining a smooth apricot juice.

4. Mix with Sugar:

- In a pitcher, combine the strained apricot juice with sugar. Stir well until the sugar is fully dissolved.

5. Add Orange Blossom Water (Optional):

- If desired, add a tablespoon of orange blossom water to enhance the aroma and flavor of the apricot juice. Stir to incorporate.

6. Chill:

    - Refrigerate the Qamar al-Din until it's well chilled.

7. Serve:

    - Serve the apricot juice over ice cubes in glasses.

8. Enjoy:

    - Enjoy the delightful and refreshing taste of Qamar al-Din, a traditional apricot juice that is popular in Middle Eastern cuisine. It's a perfect choice for a cool and flavorful beverage.

Mint Lemonade (Limonana)

Ingredients:

- 1 cup fresh lemon juice (about 4-6 lemons)
- 1 cup sugar (adjust to taste)
- 1 bunch fresh mint leaves (about 1 cup packed)
- 4 cups cold water
- Ice cubes (for serving)
- Lemon slices and mint sprigs for garnish (optional)

Instructions:

1. Make Mint Simple Syrup:

- In a saucepan, combine 1 cup of sugar with 1 cup of water over medium heat. Stir until the sugar dissolves, creating a simple syrup. Add the fresh mint leaves to the syrup and simmer for a few minutes. Remove from heat and let it cool. Strain the mint leaves, leaving you with mint-infused simple syrup.

2. Juice Lemons:

- Squeeze enough lemons to obtain 1 cup of fresh lemon juice.

3. Blend Lemon Juice and Mint Syrup:

- In a blender, combine the fresh lemon juice with the mint-infused simple syrup. Blend until well combined.

4. Strain (Optional):

- If you prefer a smoother texture, you can strain the lemon and mint mixture through a fine sieve or cheesecloth to remove any pulp.

5. Mix with Cold Water:

- Pour the lemon and mint mixture into a pitcher and add 4 cups of cold water. Stir well.

6. Adjust Sweetness:

- Taste the mint lemonade and adjust the sweetness by adding more sugar if needed.

7. Chill:

    - Refrigerate the mint lemonade for at least 1-2 hours to allow the flavors to meld and for it to become nicely chilled.

8. Serve Over Ice:

    - Pour the mint lemonade over ice cubes in glasses.

9. Garnish (Optional):

    - Garnish each glass with a slice of lemon and a sprig of fresh mint.

10. Enjoy:

    - Refresh yourself with a glass of homemade Mint Lemonade (Limonana). It's a perfect balance of citrusy, sweet, and minty flavors, making it a delightful drink for any occasion.

Grilled Dishes:

Shish Kebab

Ingredients:

For the Marinade:

- 1.5 lbs (700g) boneless meat (beef, lamb, chicken), cut into cubes
- 1/4 cup olive oil
- 3 tablespoons plain yogurt
- 2 tablespoons tomato paste
- 2 tablespoons red wine vinegar
- 2 cloves garlic, minced
- 1 teaspoon ground cumin
- 1 teaspoon ground coriander
- 1 teaspoon smoked paprika
- 1 teaspoon dried oregano
- Salt and pepper to taste

For the Skewers:

- Metal or wooden skewers (if using wooden, soak them in water for at least 30 minutes to prevent burning)

Optional Garnish:

- Lemon wedges
- Chopped fresh parsley or cilantro

Instructions:

1. Prepare the Marinade:

- In a bowl, mix together olive oil, yogurt, tomato paste, red wine vinegar, minced garlic, cumin, coriander, smoked paprika, dried oregano, salt, and pepper. This creates a flavorful marinade.

2. Marinate the Meat:

- Place the cubed meat in a large bowl or resealable plastic bag. Pour the marinade over the meat, ensuring it's well-coated. Cover and refrigerate for at least 2 hours or preferably overnight for the best flavor.

3. Preheat the Grill:

- Preheat your grill to medium-high heat.

4. Skewer the Meat:

- Thread the marinated meat cubes onto skewers, leaving a little space between each piece.

5. Grill the Kebabs:

- Grill the skewers for about 10-15 minutes, turning occasionally, until the meat is cooked to your desired level of doneness and has a nice char on the outside.

6. Serve:

- Once cooked, remove the skewers from the grill and let them rest for a few minutes.

7. Optional Garnish:

- Garnish the shish kebabs with lemon wedges and chopped fresh parsley or cilantro.

8. Enjoy:

- Serve the shish kebabs hot, either on their own or with your favorite side dishes. They pair well with rice, grilled vegetables, or flatbreads. Enjoy this delicious and classic grilled dish!

Kofta (Minced Meat Skewers)

Ingredients:

For the Kofta:

- 1.5 lbs (700g) ground meat (beef, lamb, or a combination)
- 1 large onion, finely grated or minced
- 2 cloves garlic, minced
- 1/2 cup fresh parsley, finely chopped
- 1/2 cup breadcrumbs
- 1 egg
- 1 teaspoon ground cumin
- 1 teaspoon ground coriander
- 1 teaspoon paprika
- Salt and pepper to taste

For the Skewers:

- Metal or wooden skewers (if using wooden, soak them in water for at least 30 minutes to prevent burning)

Optional Tzatziki Sauce:

- 1 cup Greek yogurt
- 1 cucumber, finely diced
- 2 cloves garlic, minced
- 1 tablespoon fresh dill, chopped
- 1 tablespoon olive oil
- Salt and pepper to taste

Instructions:

1. Prepare the Kofta Mixture:

- In a large bowl, combine ground meat, finely grated or minced onion, minced garlic, chopped fresh parsley, breadcrumbs, egg, cumin, coriander, paprika, salt, and pepper. Mix well until all ingredients are evenly incorporated.

2. Shape the Kofta:

- Take a portion of the mixture and shape it around a skewer, forming elongated meat cylinders. Repeat the process for the remaining mixture.

3. Preheat the Grill:

- Preheat your grill to medium-high heat.

4. Grill the Kofta:

- Place the kofta skewers on the preheated grill. Grill for about 12-15 minutes, turning occasionally, until the meat is cooked through and has a nice char on the outside.

5. Prepare Tzatziki Sauce (Optional):

- In a bowl, mix together Greek yogurt, finely diced cucumber, minced garlic, chopped fresh dill, olive oil, salt, and pepper to taste. This creates a refreshing tzatziki sauce to serve with the kofta.

6. Serve:

- Once the kofta skewers are cooked, remove them from the grill. Serve them hot with the optional tzatziki sauce on the side.

7. Enjoy:

- Enjoy the flavorful and juicy kofta skewers either on their own or with your preferred accompaniments like rice, salad, or flatbreads. It's a delicious and satisfying dish for any occasion!

Vegetarian Delights:

Koshari (Vegetarian Version)

Ingredients:

For the Rice:

- 1 cup white rice
- 2 cups water
- Salt to taste

For the Lentils:

- 1 cup brown lentils
- 4 cups water
- Salt to taste

For the Pasta:

- 1 cup elbow macaroni or small pasta
- Water for boiling
- Salt to taste

For the Tomato Sauce:

- 2 tablespoons olive oil
- 1 onion, finely chopped
- 3 cloves garlic, minced
- 2 cans (14 oz each) crushed tomatoes
- 1 teaspoon ground cumin
- 1 teaspoon ground coriander
- 1/2 teaspoon cayenne pepper (optional, for heat)
- Salt and pepper to taste

For the Chickpeas:

- 1 can (15 oz) chickpeas, drained and rinsed

For the Fried Onions:

- 1 large onion, thinly sliced
- Vegetable oil for frying

For Serving (Optional):

- Chopped fresh parsley
- Vinegar-based hot sauce

Instructions:

1. Prepare Rice:

- In a saucepan, combine 1 cup of rice with 2 cups of water and salt. Bring to a boil, then reduce heat, cover, and simmer until the rice is cooked. Fluff the rice with a fork.

2. Cook Lentils:

- In a separate pot, combine brown lentils with 4 cups of water and salt. Bring to a boil, then reduce heat and simmer until the lentils are tender but not mushy. Drain any excess water.

3. Boil Pasta:

- Cook the elbow macaroni or small pasta in boiling salted water according to package instructions. Drain and set aside.

4. Prepare Tomato Sauce:

- In a saucepan, heat olive oil over medium heat. Add chopped onions and garlic, sauté until softened. Add crushed tomatoes, cumin, coriander, cayenne pepper (if using), salt, and pepper. Simmer for about 15-20 minutes, stirring occasionally.

5. Prepare Chickpeas:

- Drain and rinse the chickpeas.

6. Fry Onions:

- In a separate pan, heat vegetable oil over medium-high heat. Fry thinly sliced onions until golden brown and crispy. Remove and place them on a paper towel to drain excess oil.

7. Assemble Koshari:

- In individual serving bowls, layer the cooked rice, lentils, pasta, chickpeas, and tomato sauce. Top with fried onions.

8. Garnish:

- Garnish with chopped fresh parsley and serve with a side of vinegar-based hot sauce if desired.

9. Enjoy:

- Mix all the components together and enjoy this delicious and hearty vegetarian version of Koshari!

Lentil Kebabs (Kebdet Adas)

Ingredients:

- 1 cup dried brown or green lentils
- 3 cups water (for cooking lentils)
- 1 large onion, finely chopped
- 3 cloves garlic, minced
- 1 cup breadcrumbs
- 1 teaspoon ground cumin
- 1 teaspoon ground coriander
- 1 teaspoon paprika
- 1/2 teaspoon cayenne pepper (adjust to taste)
- Salt and pepper to taste
- 2 tablespoons olive oil (plus extra for brushing)
- Fresh parsley, chopped (for garnish)

Instructions:

1. Cook Lentils:

- Rinse the lentils thoroughly and place them in a pot with 3 cups of water. Bring to a boil, then reduce heat and simmer until the lentils are tender but not mushy. Drain any excess water.

2. Sauté Onion and Garlic:

- In a pan, heat 2 tablespoons of olive oil over medium heat. Sauté chopped onions until translucent, then add minced garlic and cook until fragrant.

3. Blend Lentils:

- In a food processor, combine the cooked lentils, sautéed onion and garlic, breadcrumbs, ground cumin, ground coriander, paprika, cayenne pepper, salt, and pepper. Blend until you get a well-combined mixture.

4. Form Kebabs:

- Take portions of the lentil mixture and shape them into kebabs or patties. If the mixture is too wet, you can add more breadcrumbs to help bind the kebabs.

5. Grill or Pan-Fry:

- You can either grill the lentil kebabs on an outdoor grill or cook them on a stovetop grill pan. Brush the kebabs with olive oil before cooking. Cook until they develop a golden-brown crust on both sides.

6. Serve:

- Arrange the lentil kebabs on a serving platter. Garnish with freshly chopped parsley.

7. Enjoy:

- Serve the Lentil Kebabs (Kebdet Adas) with your favorite dipping sauce or enjoy them in a pita as a vegetarian kebab sandwich. They are flavorful, protein-packed, and make a delicious and healthy meatless option.

Traditional Sweets:

Roz Bel Laban (Rice Pudding)

Ingredients:

- 1/2 cup short-grain rice (such as Arborio)
- 4 cups whole milk
- 1/2 cup sugar (adjust to taste)
- 1/2 teaspoon vanilla extract
- Pinch of salt
- Ground cinnamon for garnish

Instructions:

1. Rinse the Rice:

- Rinse the short-grain rice under cold water until the water runs clear. This helps remove excess starch.

2. Cook the Rice:

- In a medium-sized, heavy-bottomed saucepan, combine the rinsed rice and 2 cups of whole milk. Cook over medium heat, stirring frequently to prevent sticking, until the rice is partially cooked.

3. Add Remaining Milk:

- Pour in the remaining 2 cups of whole milk, stir well, and bring the mixture to a gentle simmer.

4. Simmer:

- Reduce the heat to low, cover the saucepan, and let the rice simmer, stirring occasionally, until it becomes soft and the mixture thickens. This may take about 30-40 minutes.

5. Add Sugar and Flavorings:

   - Once the rice is cooked and the mixture has thickened, add sugar, vanilla extract, and a pinch of salt. Stir well to combine.

6. Continue Cooking:

   - Continue cooking the rice pudding over low heat, stirring frequently, until the sugar is completely dissolved, and the pudding reaches your desired consistency.

7. Remove from Heat:

   - Remove the saucepan from heat and let the rice pudding cool slightly.

8. Serve Warm or Chilled:

   - You can serve Roz Bel Laban warm or chilled, depending on your preference. If serving chilled, transfer the pudding to serving bowls and refrigerate for a few hours.

9. Garnish:

   - Before serving, sprinkle ground cinnamon over the top for a classic garnish.

10. Enjoy:

    - Enjoy this creamy and comforting Roz Bel Laban as a delightful dessert. It's a traditional rice pudding that is loved for its simplicity and rich flavor.

Basbousa with Pistachios

Ingredients:

For the Basbousa:

- 1 cup semolina
- 1 cup granulated sugar
- 1 cup plain yogurt
- 1/2 cup unsalted butter, melted
- 1 teaspoon baking powder
- 1/2 cup desiccated coconut
- 1/4 cup milk
- 1 teaspoon vanilla extract
- 1/4 cup finely ground pistachios (for batter)
- 1/4 cup chopped pistachios (for garnish)

For the Sugar Syrup:

- 1 cup granulated sugar
- 1/2 cup water
- 1 tablespoon lemon juice
- 1 teaspoon rose water or orange blossom water (optional)

Instructions:

1. Preheat Oven:

   - Preheat your oven to 350°F (175°C). Grease a baking dish or line it with parchment paper.

2. Prepare Basbousa Batter:

   - In a large mixing bowl, combine semolina, sugar, yogurt, melted butter, baking powder, desiccated coconut, milk, vanilla extract, and finely ground pistachios. Mix until well combined.

3. Rest the Batter:

- Allow the basbousa batter to rest for about 10-15 minutes. This helps the semolina absorb the liquids.

4. Pour Batter into Baking Dish:

    - Pour the rested basbousa batter into the prepared baking dish, spreading it evenly.

5. Bake:

    - Bake in the preheated oven for approximately 30-40 minutes or until the top is golden brown and a toothpick inserted into the center comes out clean.

6. Prepare Sugar Syrup:

    - While the basbousa is baking, prepare the sugar syrup. In a saucepan, combine sugar, water, and lemon juice. Bring to a boil, then reduce heat and simmer for about 10 minutes. Add rose water or orange blossom water if using. Allow the syrup to cool.

7. Cut and Pour Syrup:

    - Once the basbousa is out of the oven, cut it into squares or diamond shapes. Pour the cooled sugar syrup over the hot basbousa, allowing it to soak in.

8. Garnish:

    - Sprinkle chopped pistachios over the top for garnish.

9. Allow to Cool:

    - Allow the basbousa to cool and absorb the syrup before serving.

10. Serve:

    - Serve the Basbousa with Pistachios at room temperature. It's a delightful Middle Eastern dessert with a moist texture and a nutty flavor from the pistachios. Enjoy!

Atayef (Stuffed Pancakes)

Ingredients:

For the Atayef:

- 2 cups all-purpose flour
- 2 tablespoons semolina
- 1 teaspoon baking powder
- 2 tablespoons sugar
- 1/2 teaspoon instant yeast
- 1.5 to 2 cups lukewarm water

For the Ashta (Cream) Filling:

- 2 cups whole milk
- 2 tablespoons cornstarch
- 1/2 cup sugar
- 1 teaspoon rose water or orange blossom water (optional)

For the Nut Filling:

- 1 cup mixed nuts (walnuts, pistachios, almonds), finely chopped
- 2 tablespoons sugar
- 1 teaspoon ground cinnamon

For Frying:

- Vegetable oil or ghee

For Garnish:

- Powdered sugar
- Crushed pistachios

Instructions:

1. Prepare the Atayef Batter:

   - In a bowl, combine the all-purpose flour, semolina, baking powder, sugar, and instant yeast. Gradually add lukewarm water while whisking until you achieve a thick pancake batter consistency. Cover and let it rest for 30 minutes.

2. Cook the Ashta (Cream) Filling:

   - In a saucepan, mix cornstarch with a small amount of milk to form a smooth paste. Add the remaining milk and sugar. Cook over medium heat, stirring constantly until the mixture thickens. Remove from heat and add rose water or orange blossom water if using. Let it cool.

3. Prepare the Nut Filling:

   - In a bowl, combine the finely chopped mixed nuts with sugar and ground cinnamon. Set aside.

4. Cook Atayef:

   - Heat a non-stick pan over medium heat. Pour small circles of the batter onto the pan, like mini pancakes. Cook until bubbles form on the surface, then flip and cook the other side briefly. You want them to be cooked on one side only.

5. Fill the Atayef:

   - For the cream-filled Atayef, place a spoonful of the ashta filling in the center of each atayef. Fold in half to create a half-moon shape and press the edges to seal.
   - For the nut-filled Atayef, place a spoonful of the nut filling in the center, fold in half, and pinch the edges to seal.

6. Fry the Atayef:

   - Heat vegetable oil or ghee in a pan. Fry the filled atayef until they are golden brown on both sides.

7. Drain and Garnish:

- Remove the fried atayef and place them on paper towels to drain excess oil. Dust with powdered sugar and sprinkle crushed pistachios on top.

8. Serve:

- Serve Atayef warm as a delightful dessert during special occasions or festive celebrations. Enjoy!

Kunafa with Nuts

Ingredients:

For the Kunafa Dough:

- 1 package (500g) kunafa dough (shredded phyllo dough)
- 1 cup unsalted butter, melted

For the Nut Filling:

- 1 cup mixed nuts (pistachios, almonds, walnuts), finely chopped
- 1/4 cup sugar
- 1 teaspoon ground cinnamon

For the Sugar Syrup:

- 1 cup sugar
- 1/2 cup water
- 1 teaspoon lemon juice
- 1 teaspoon rose water or orange blossom water (optional)

Instructions:

1. Prepare the Nut Filling:

- In a bowl, mix the finely chopped mixed nuts with sugar and ground cinnamon. Set aside.

2. Prepare the Sugar Syrup:

- In a saucepan, combine sugar, water, and lemon juice. Bring to a boil, then reduce heat and simmer for about 10 minutes until the syrup slightly thickens. Add rose water or orange blossom water if using. Allow the syrup to cool.

3. Prepare the Kunafa Dough:

- Preheat your oven to 350°F (175°C). Brush a baking dish with melted butter.
- In a large bowl, separate the strands of the kunafa dough. Pour melted butter over the strands and toss them gently to ensure they are all coated.

4. Assemble the Kunafa:

- Take half of the kunafa strands and press them into the bottom of the prepared baking dish to form an even layer. Press the layer down firmly.
- Sprinkle the nut filling evenly over the first layer of kunafa.
- Top the nut filling with the remaining half of the kunafa strands. Press down gently to form another even layer.
- Drizzle any remaining melted butter over the top layer.

5. Bake:

- Bake in the preheated oven for 30-40 minutes or until the kunafa turns golden brown and crispy.

6. Pour Sugar Syrup:

- Remove the kunafa from the oven and immediately pour the cooled sugar syrup evenly over the hot kunafa. Allow the syrup to be absorbed.

7. Cool and Slice:

- Allow the kunafa to cool for a while before slicing it into squares or diamonds.

8. Serve:

- Serve the Kunafa with Nuts at room temperature. It's a delightful dessert with a crispy texture, sweet nutty filling, and aromatic sugar syrup. Enjoy!

Seafood Specialities:

Sayadiya (Fish and Rice Dish)

Ingredients:

For the Rice:

- 2 cups basmati rice
- 4 cups water
- 1 onion, finely chopped
- 2 tablespoons vegetable oil
- 1 teaspoon ground cumin
- 1 teaspoon ground coriander
- Salt to taste

For the Fish:

- 1.5 lbs (700g) white fish fillets (such as tilapia or cod)
- 2 onions, thinly sliced
- 3 cloves garlic, minced
- 2 tablespoons vegetable oil
- 1 teaspoon ground cumin
- 1 teaspoon ground coriander
- 1 teaspoon ground cinnamon
- 1 teaspoon paprika
- Salt and pepper to taste
- Juice of 1 lemon

For the Caramelized Onion Topping:

- 2 large onions, thinly sliced
- Vegetable oil for frying

Instructions:

1. Prepare the Rice:

- Rinse the basmati rice under cold water until the water runs clear. In a pot, sauté the chopped onion in vegetable oil until translucent. Add ground cumin, ground coriander, and salt. Stir for a minute.
- Add the rinsed rice to the pot and stir to coat the rice with the spices and onions. Pour in the water and bring to a boil. Reduce heat, cover, and simmer until the rice is cooked.

2. Prepare the Fish:

- In a separate pan, sauté the sliced onions in vegetable oil until golden brown. Add minced garlic and continue to sauté until fragrant.
- Season the fish fillets with ground cumin, ground coriander, ground cinnamon, paprika, salt, and pepper. Place the seasoned fish on top of the sautéed onions and garlic. Squeeze lemon juice over the fish.
- Cover the pan and let the fish cook over medium heat until it's done. Be careful not to overcook the fish; it should be flaky and tender.

3. Prepare the Caramelized Onion Topping:

- In a separate pan, heat vegetable oil and fry thinly sliced onions until deep golden brown and caramelized. Drain excess oil.

4. Assemble Sayadiya:

- Once the rice and fish are cooked, place a layer of rice on a serving platter. Top it with the cooked fish and the caramelized onion topping.

5. Serve:

- Serve Sayadiya hot, with the flavors of the spiced rice complementing the tender fish, and the caramelized onions adding a sweet and savory touch. Enjoy!

Fried Fish with Tarator Sauce

Ingredients:

For the Fried Fish:

- 1.5 lbs (700g) white fish fillets (such as tilapia or cod)
- 1 cup all-purpose flour
- 2 eggs, beaten
- Salt and pepper to taste
- Vegetable oil for frying

For the Tarator Sauce:

- 1 cup tahini
- 3 cloves garlic, minced
- 1/4 cup lemon juice
- 1/4 cup water
- Salt to taste
- Chopped fresh parsley for garnish

Instructions:

1. Prepare the Tarator Sauce:

- In a bowl, whisk together tahini, minced garlic, lemon juice, and water until you get a smooth and creamy consistency. Add salt to taste. Adjust the thickness by adding more water if needed.
- Set aside the tarator sauce and allow the flavors to meld.

2. Fry the Fish:

- In a shallow dish, season the all-purpose flour with salt and pepper. Dredge each fish fillet in the seasoned flour, coating it evenly.
- Dip the floured fish fillets into the beaten eggs, ensuring they are well-coated.

- In a skillet, heat vegetable oil over medium-high heat. Fry the fish fillets until they are golden brown and cooked through, about 3-4 minutes per side, depending on the thickness of the fillets. Ensure the internal temperature reaches 145°F (63°C).
- Place the fried fish on a plate lined with paper towels to absorb any excess oil.

3. Serve:

- Arrange the fried fish on a serving platter. Drizzle the tarator sauce over the top or serve it on the side for dipping.

4. Garnish:

- Garnish the dish with chopped fresh parsley for a burst of color and flavor.

5. Enjoy:

- Serve the Fried Fish with Tarator Sauce immediately while the fish is still crispy and hot. The creamy and tangy tarator sauce complements the fried fish, creating a delicious and satisfying dish. Enjoy!

Special Occasion Dishes:

Mulukhiyah with Rabbit

Ingredients:

For the Mulukhiyah:

- 2 cups dried mulukhiyah leaves (jute leaves), cleaned and chopped
- 1.5 lbs (700g) rabbit meat, cleaned and cut into pieces
- 1 large onion, finely chopped
- 4 cloves garlic, minced
- 2 tablespoons vegetable oil
- 1 teaspoon ground coriander
- 1 teaspoon ground cumin
- 1 teaspoon ground cinnamon
- Salt and pepper to taste
- 8 cups chicken or rabbit broth
- Juice of 1 lemon

For the Rice:

- 2 cups white rice
- 4 cups water
- Salt to taste

For Garnish:

- Vegetable oil for frying
- Chopped fresh cilantro or parsley

Instructions:

1. Prepare the Mulukhiyah:

- In a large pot, heat vegetable oil over medium heat. Sauté the chopped onions until translucent, then add minced garlic and continue sautéing until fragrant.
- Add the rabbit pieces to the pot and brown them on all sides.
- Season the rabbit with ground coriander, ground cumin, ground cinnamon, salt, and pepper. Stir well to coat the rabbit with the spices.
- Pour in the chicken or rabbit broth, bring to a boil, then reduce the heat and let it simmer until the rabbit is tender. This may take around 45 minutes to an hour.
- Once the rabbit is cooked, add the chopped mulukhiyah leaves to the pot. Simmer for an additional 15-20 minutes until the mulukhiyah is cooked and tender.
- Stir in the lemon juice and adjust the seasoning if needed.

2. Prepare the Rice:

- Rinse the rice under cold water until the water runs clear. In a pot, bring water to a boil. Add salt and the rinsed rice. Cook the rice according to package instructions until fluffy and tender.

3. Fry the Garnish:

- In a separate pan, heat vegetable oil for frying. Fry the chopped cilantro or parsley until crispy. Drain on paper towels.

4. Serve:

- Serve the mulukhiyah with rabbit over a bed of rice. Drizzle some of the broth over the rice and rabbit.

5. Garnish and Enjoy:

- Sprinkle the fried cilantro or parsley over the top as a garnish. Enjoy your Mulukhiyah with Rabbit, a hearty and flavorful dish with the unique taste of mulukhiyah leaves.

Fattah with Lamb

Ingredients:

For the Lamb:

- 1.5 lbs (700g) lamb, cubed
- 1 large onion, finely chopped
- 3 cloves garlic, minced
- 2 tablespoons vegetable oil
- 1 teaspoon ground cumin
- 1 teaspoon ground coriander
- 1 teaspoon ground cinnamon
- Salt and pepper to taste
- 4 cups water

For the Rice:

- 2 cups white rice
- 4 cups lamb or vegetable broth (from cooking lamb)
- Salt to taste

For the Bread:

- 4 pieces of flatbread or pita, torn into bite-sized pieces
- Vegetable oil for frying

For the Yogurt Sauce:

- 2 cups Greek yogurt
- 2 cloves garlic, minced
- Salt to taste

For Garnish:

- Pine nuts, toasted
- Chopped fresh parsley

Instructions:

1. Cook the Lamb:

    - In a large pot, heat vegetable oil over medium heat. Sauté chopped onions until translucent, then add minced garlic and cook until fragrant.
    - Add cubed lamb to the pot and brown it on all sides.
    - Season the lamb with ground cumin, ground coriander, ground cinnamon, salt, and pepper. Stir well to coat the lamb with the spices.
    - Pour in 4 cups of water, bring to a boil, then reduce the heat and let it simmer until the lamb is tender. This may take around 1 to 1.5 hours. Adjust the seasoning if needed.

2. Prepare the Rice:

    - Rinse the white rice under cold water until the water runs clear. In a separate pot, cook the rice in lamb or vegetable broth (taken from cooking lamb) with salt according to package instructions until done.

3. Fry the Bread:

    - Heat vegetable oil in a pan. Fry the torn flatbread or pita pieces until golden brown and crispy. Drain on paper towels.

4. Prepare the Yogurt Sauce:

    - In a bowl, mix Greek yogurt with minced garlic and salt. Adjust the seasoning to taste.

5. Assemble the Fattah:

    - On a serving platter, arrange a layer of cooked rice. Place the cooked lamb on top of the rice.
    - Pour some of the lamb broth over the rice and lamb to moisten it.
    - Spread the fried bread pieces over the top.
    - Drizzle the yogurt sauce over the bread.

6. Garnish:

    - Garnish the Fattah with toasted pine nuts and chopped fresh parsley.

7. Serve:

- Serve Fattah with Lamb warm. The combination of tender lamb, flavorful rice, crispy bread, and creamy yogurt sauce creates a rich and satisfying dish. Enjoy!

Spicy Delicacies:

Hawawshi (Spicy Meat Pie)

Ingredients:

For the Dough:

- 4 cups all-purpose flour
- 1 cup warm water
- 1 teaspoon salt
- 2 tablespoons vegetable oil

For the Filling:

- 1 lb (450g) ground beef or lamb
- 1 onion, finely chopped
- 2 tomatoes, finely chopped
- 1/4 cup chopped fresh parsley
- 2 cloves garlic, minced
- 1 teaspoon ground cumin
- 1 teaspoon ground coriander
- 1 teaspoon paprika
- 1 teaspoon cayenne pepper (adjust to taste)
- Salt and pepper to taste

For Assembling:

- Butter or ghee for brushing

Instructions:

1. Prepare the Dough:

- In a large bowl, combine the flour, warm water, salt, and vegetable oil. Knead the mixture until you have a smooth and elastic dough. Cover and let it rest for about 30 minutes.

2. Prepare the Filling:

- In a mixing bowl, combine ground beef or lamb with finely chopped onions, tomatoes, parsley, minced garlic, ground cumin, ground coriander, paprika, cayenne pepper, salt, and pepper. Mix well until the ingredients are evenly distributed.

3. Preheat the Oven:

- Preheat your oven to 400°F (200°C).

4. Assemble the Hawawshi:

- Divide the dough into equal-sized portions. Roll each portion into a thin round sheet, similar to the size of a small pizza.
- Place a generous amount of the prepared meat filling on one half of each dough round, leaving a border around the edges.
- Fold the other half of the dough over the filling, creating a semi-circle. Press the edges firmly to seal.

5. Bake:

- Place the assembled hawawshi on a baking sheet. Brush the tops with melted butter or ghee.
- Bake in the preheated oven for about 15-20 minutes or until the dough is golden brown and the filling is cooked through.

6. Serve:

- Slice the hawawshi into wedges and serve while warm. It's delicious on its own or served with tahini sauce or your favorite condiments.

7. Enjoy:

- Enjoy the Hawawshi as a flavorful and spicy meat pie, perfect for a hearty snack or a main course.

Kebsa (Spicy Rice with Meat)

Ingredients:

For the Rice:

- 2 cups basmati rice
- 4 cups water
- 2 tablespoons vegetable oil
- 1 onion, finely chopped
- 2 tomatoes, diced
- 3 cloves garlic, minced
- 1 teaspoon ground cumin
- 1 teaspoon ground coriander
- 1 teaspoon ground cinnamon
- 1 teaspoon ground cardamom
- Salt to taste

For the Meat:

- 1.5 lbs (700g) chicken or lamb, cut into pieces
- 2 tablespoons vegetable oil
- 1 onion, finely chopped
- 2 tablespoons tomato paste
- 1 teaspoon ground cumin
- 1 teaspoon ground coriander
- 1 teaspoon ground cinnamon
- 1 teaspoon ground cardamom
- Salt and pepper to taste

For Garnish:

- Chopped fresh cilantro or parsley
- Almonds or pine nuts, toasted

Instructions:

1. Prepare the Rice:

- Rinse the basmati rice under cold water until the water runs clear. In a pot, heat vegetable oil over medium heat. Sauté chopped onions until translucent, then add minced garlic and diced tomatoes. Cook until the tomatoes are soft.
- Add ground cumin, ground coriander, ground cinnamon, ground cardamom, and salt. Stir well to combine.
- Add the rinsed rice to the pot and stir to coat the rice with the spices and vegetables. Pour in water and bring to a boil. Reduce heat, cover, and simmer until the rice is cooked.

2. Prepare the Meat:

- In a separate pan, heat vegetable oil over medium heat. Sauté chopped onions until golden brown. Add the chicken or lamb pieces and brown them on all sides.
- Stir in tomato paste, ground cumin, ground coriander, ground cinnamon, ground cardamom, salt, and pepper. Cook until the meat is fully cooked.

3. Combine Rice and Meat:

- Once both the rice and meat are cooked, combine them in a large serving dish. Mix gently to evenly distribute the meat throughout the spiced rice.

4. Garnish:

- Garnish the Kebsa with chopped fresh cilantro or parsley and toasted almonds or pine nuts.

5. Serve:

- Serve Kebsa hot, with the aromatic blend of spices infusing the rice and meat. Enjoy this flavorful and satisfying dish with your favorite condiments on the side.

Shatta (Hot Pepper Sauce)

Ingredients:

- 10-15 hot red chili peppers (such as Fresno or Thai chilies), stems removed
- 4 cloves garlic, peeled
- 1 teaspoon ground coriander
- 1 teaspoon ground cumin
- 1 teaspoon salt
- 1/2 cup olive oil
- Juice of 1 lemon

Instructions:

1. Prepare the Peppers:

- Wear gloves to protect your hands from the heat of the peppers. Remove the stems from the chili peppers.

2. Blend Ingredients:

- In a blender or food processor, combine the chili peppers, peeled garlic cloves, ground coriander, ground cumin, and salt.
- Blend the ingredients until you get a coarse paste. You can adjust the texture by blending more or less, depending on your preference.

3. Add Olive Oil:

- With the blender or food processor running, slowly drizzle in the olive oil until the mixture emulsifies into a smooth sauce.

4. Adjust Seasoning:

- Taste the shatta and adjust the salt if necessary. You can also add more lemon juice for acidity if desired.

5. Store:

- Transfer the shatta to a clean, airtight jar or container. Seal it well and store it in the refrigerator.

6. Serve:

- Shatta is a versatile hot sauce that can be used to add heat and flavor to a variety of dishes. Serve it alongside grilled meats, falafel, sandwiches, or any other dish that could use a spicy kick.

7. Enjoy:

- Enjoy the intense heat and bold flavors of homemade shatta! Adjust the spiciness by varying the number of chili peppers or adding different varieties to suit your taste.

Miscellaneous:

Aish Merahrah (Red Lentil Bread)

Ingredients:

For the Red Lentil Paste:

- 1 cup red lentils, washed and soaked for at least 2 hours
- 1 cup water
- 2 cloves garlic, minced
- 1 teaspoon ground cumin
- 1 teaspoon ground coriander
- Salt to taste

For the Bread Dough:

- 3 cups all-purpose flour
- 1 tablespoon sugar
- 1 tablespoon active dry yeast
- 1 cup warm water
- 2 tablespoons olive oil
- 1 teaspoon salt

Instructions:

1. Prepare the Red Lentil Paste:

- In a saucepan, combine red lentils, water, minced garlic, ground cumin, ground coriander, and salt. Cook over medium heat until the lentils are soft and the mixture forms a thick paste. Let it cool.

2. Activate the Yeast:

- In a bowl, combine warm water, sugar, and active dry yeast. Let it sit for about 5-10 minutes until the yeast becomes frothy.

3. Make the Bread Dough:

- In a large mixing bowl, combine the all-purpose flour and salt. Add the red lentil paste, activated yeast mixture, and olive oil.

- Knead the mixture to form a soft and elastic dough. You can adjust the consistency by adding more flour if needed.

4. Let the Dough Rise:

- Place the dough in a lightly oiled bowl, cover it with a damp cloth, and let it rise in a warm place for about 1-2 hours or until it doubles in size.

5. Shape the Bread:

- Preheat your oven to 400°F (200°C). Punch down the risen dough and divide it into equal portions. Shape each portion into a round or oval shape.

6. Bake:

- Place the shaped dough on a baking sheet or in a baking dish. Bake in the preheated oven for 15-20 minutes or until the bread is golden brown and cooked through.

7. Serve:

- Let the Aish Merahrah cool for a few minutes before slicing. Serve it warm with your favorite dips, spreads, or as a side to complement your meals.

8. Enjoy:

- Enjoy the unique flavor and added nutritional benefits of red lentils in this delicious Aish Merahrah. It's a delightful and wholesome bread option.

www.ingramcontent.com/pod-product-compliance
Lightning Source LLC
LaVergne TN
LVHW081552060526
838201LV00054B/1877